Getting Your House In Order

Getting Your House In Order

Mary Jane Preston

PARACLETE PRESS
ORLEANS, MASSACHUSETTS

Fourth Printing, October 1990

© 1985 by Mary Jane Preston
Library of Congress #: 85-61715
ISBN: 0-941478-48-3
All rights reserved.
Published by Paraclete Press
Orleans, Massachusetts
Printed in the United States of America

Table of Contents

Getting This Book in Order

You know how it feels when you keep putting a job off, planning to do it but never quite taking the time to get started? That's where this book began. For several years, friends had been urging me to write it, and finally I even admitted that I felt God nudging me in the same direction. But what should I do first? There I was, the person doing a book about how to be organized, and I couldn't even get myself moving.

Finally, one weekend on a women's retreat, a whole morning was set aside for us to work on something creative. I had brought a notebook and knew it was time to start by writing about how to use a schedule and do spring cleaning. I was ready! But when they read off the list of assigned areas, I suddenly heard my name in the Cake Decorating group. Was this a trick? I had been so certain that God had set this time aside for me to get started! There I sat, mumbling under my breath. No way did I want to get into batter and icing! The people around me knew I was angry, and the woman next to me tried to calm me down by whispering that maybe I could ask to be switched. I knew I should be open to God's direction, but I was so sure I was supposed to write . . . .

My thoughts were interrupted by the retreat leader again reading my name — and this time in the Writing Group! "Oh," she said, looking up, "I guess that was Mary Jackson, not you, Mary Jane, in the cake group." Thank you, Lord! I was on my way to a morning of writing.

I sat staring at a nice white paper and a list of seven topics. My mind felt empty — where should I start, who was I talking to, what would really help people? Beverly, one of the other "writers," and I were supposed to pray together — so that was the first step. I asked the Lord to be in charge of the whole project — to show me what He wanted me to do. Then I waited for inspiration. Almost immediately a plan of attack began to take shape in my mind, and the ideas came so fast that I had trouble getting them all down. I had intended to make a neat, orderly outline, but soon forgot that, as I furiously jotted down ideas and examples all over the margins. By lunchtime, I had five pages of scribbled notes, and as I looked at them, I was filled with a sense of awe — there really *was* a book here! I said a silent prayer of thanks, because I knew that I never could have done it without His help; in fact, it felt at times almost like He was pushing my pen.

The awareness that God was in the project, and that it could help people, filled me with a sense of purpose and excitement. *But* — knowing myself, and how I had procrastinated on beginning the book, I sought out a friend on the retreat and committed myself out loud to her, to write the first chapter the following week.

With a start like that, you would think that I would be off and running, right? Wrong. Several weeks later, an outline and a chapter were *still* all I had. Talk about writer's block, I was at a dead end, and I had barely gotten started! A close friend thought I ought to send what I had to a book editor I knew for suggestions. Maybe he could help me see where I was going. Good! I could mail it off and forget about it, for awhile.

One morning, a week later, I received a call at the office where I work. It was the editor, saying he and his company thought my book idea was a natural that would speak to a great many people, and they wanted to publish it. I sat at my desk dumbfounded.

"You will need to set a schedule for yourself," the editor went on, "and a target date to finish the first draft." The words washed over me, as I tried to make appropriate responses. "If you possibly can, I think you should write at least two hours a day, and send the first draft to me by Easter."

What are you *talking* about, I thought; it is already the first week of Lent! *Two hours a day* — I have three part-time jobs, plus my family, and church activities. What do you think I *am*? My emotions were a tumbled mixture of pride, terror, and anger. All of which, I tried to keep hidden. "Well, sure. . . okay. . . um, I guess so."

He continued to make suggestions on how to proceed, and all at once he came up with a whole new idea: "The person reading your book won't have any idea who you are. Why should he or she listen to your ideas on how to organize a home? You need to let your readers know who you are and how you react. You'd better give them your own story at the beginning, and be dead-honest, even if it means showing how much you don't have it all together. If you're *that* honest, they'll trust you. Because you're no different from them."

Now on a speaker's platform, I've never minded sharing stories about myself — dumb things I have done, ways that God has touched my life, little slices of what goes on at our house . . . but tell my *whole* story in the first chapter? To a reader I didn't know and *couldn't* see? That was more than a little scary!

When the phone conversation ended, I sat there just staring at the phone for more than a minute. Then I jumped up to share my news with my co-workers, I was off and running, scared and excited, towards my Easter goal. God certainly had chosen an unexpected Lenten discipline for me!

Now, it is five months later, and it's done. This book, which deep down I never really thought would happen, has come to pass. All I did was follow the system: first, step back and assess the existing situation. Then, establish what I wanted to accomplish, and what it would take to get the manuscript done within the time frame available. Next, I had to differentiate between what must be done, what would be nice to get done, and what didn't have to be done within that time frame. And finally, I had to set up a realistic schedule.

There was (and is) one other ingredient: many times you will face, as I did, a situtation, time frame, or ultimate goal that is simply impossible, no matter how you break it down and analyze it. Natural man (or woman) cannot cope with it. But we have supernatural help awaiting our call, and we need to avail ourselves of it. Among other things, the first chapter will tell how I discovered this secret ingredient, and what a difference it has made.

The rest of this workbook is just that: a systematic workbook which will guide you to a new understanding of what it will take to bring order into your home — and peace (and dare we say, joy?) into your heart. After the first chapter, you'll need a pen or favorite writing implement, and I would urge you not to skip any of the blanks, as you go. Fill each one in, and I suspect you'll find, as I have, that it will show you a great deal about yourself, as well as give you a fresh outlook on your home — and your life.

Mary Jane Preston
Rochester, New York

1

Nothing Is Impossible

So, where does one start, in baring one's life to a perfect stranger? I am the oldest of four children in my family — a leader from day one. I was usually confident I could succeed, and I just knew everyone was fascinated by all the things I had to say. As a gregarious teenager, I babbled through dinner about the activities of my day, barely giving anyone else a chance to join in. It was a family joke that I even managed to talk while I took breaths, afraid that someone else would start talking, if I stopped for a few seconds.

In school, I worked hard to excel and loved the compliments and attention that it brought. Early on, I had found my groove: I never hesitated to volunteer for extra credit work, or to write a 40-page paper, when 25 pages were all that was required.

In my group of friends, I was always striving to be the best — and always falling a little short. For instance, I was co-captain of the varsity basketball team, but felt destroyed that I never made the cheerleading squad. I usually had a boyfriend, but was never the May Queen type. Once, I remember sitting crumpled up on my parents' bathroom floor, crying my eyes out after a boy had broken up with me. I was sure my younger, very popular, brother would be embarrassed to have a "rejected" sister. And somehow, getting straight A's was never quite enough. My mother often had to comfort me, when I came home after school, devastated about a 95% on a test when a friend (or even worse, my brother) had gotten a 99%.

I loved being active, joining many clubs and teams. Our high school wasn't large, and as we were the first graduating class, we got to do everything. I ran from hockey practice, to yearbook staff meetings, to Future Teachers of America, to Girl Scouts, to Leaders' Club. I couldn't stand to be left out of anything!

But that was my public face; at home, things were a little different. I was a pro at talking back to my parents, a great one for arguing my case and proving I was right. My biggest concerns were *myself*, *my* friends, *my* school work, *my* activities. I certainly didn't think I should have to do much around the house. Dusting, ironing, cleaning bathrooms — I was too busy. And anyway, my mother was a full-time homemaker; that was her job. I made my bed and kept my room picked up. Wasn't that enough? Of course, I was supposed to help with the dishes, but amazingly, I would often feel the "call of nature," just as the glasses were being done, and return (after flipping through a whole issue of *Saturday Evening Post*) in time to dry the last few pots and pans.

I never offered to help get dinner ready — I was taking a break from homework to watch "Spin and Marty" on the Mickey Mouse Club and wondering if the meal would be on time — I was hungry. I never went out of my way to do anything for anybody — unless I thought company was coming, and I wanted to show off a little. I rarely did any more than the bare minimum that was required of me.

But looking back, the thing I'm most ashamed of was the way I was disrespectful to my parents. My mother and I talked and shared a lot, but when I was upset, she bore the brunt of it. I hated having to help fold sheets when I came home from school, and my anger often spilled out in smart remarks. I wanted to be soothed and reassured that I was doing things right, and if Mom tried to steer me in a better direction, I would blow up — storming upstairs, mumbling "I hate you" under my breath and slamming my bedroom door.

My father enjoyed books on how to lead a better Christian life. For some reason, which was unfathomable to me, he liked to have me sit on the foot of his bed in the evening, so he could read them aloud to me. I hated it — it took too long and the subject made me feel embarrassed. One of my less endearing habits was giggling at inappropriate moments, when it was supposed to be serious and uplifting. I was definitely not into that religious stuff. I was doing quite well on my own, and anyway, homework was much more important. As I avoided eye contact by staring at the sheets, my face would get covered with pink blotches, and I would wait for the end of the chapter, desparately trying not to giggle. "Well, Dad, that's interesting, and all, but, um . . . well, I've got a history test tomorrow, and I really need to study for it now." Then I would beat a hasty retreat to the comfort and privacy of my own room.

My family belonged to a Presbyterian church, and were deeply involved there. My father served on the session and was Sunday School superintendent, while the Women's Association and their annual bazaar took a lot of my mother's time. We went every Sunday — no matter what! If I had been babysitting until 3 A.M. Sunday morning, Dad still pried me out of bed for church. I enjoyed being with my friends in the youth group and choir, but I was always impatient sitting through church, and often passed the time jotting down lists of things I had to do, or making faces about the sermon with my younger brother.

I never made any kind of religious commitment. Being a Presbyterian was enough, and I never really wanted anything deeper. Our minister or youth worker may have talked about giving one's life to Christ, but if they did, I wasn't on that wave length. Checking out the whole scene with the "know-it-all" eyes of youth, I made a few decisions: I would never join a woman's circle; it took too much time and sounded boring. And looking at how hard my mother and father worked, and how little they were appreciated, as far as I could see, I promised myself that no one would ever "use" me. In fact, the whole Christian thing seemed not worth the effort. I wanted some kind of reward, a place of importance, not just a lot of hard work for nothing.

But except for tears over broken relationships, cheerleading tryouts and making less than perfect grades, my high school years were full of happy memories. And all the time, I was dashing toward my next goal: college. I had plans for my life! I wasn't going to be "just a housewife" — I was going to be a teacher, and just maybe the best one ever! Someday I hoped to be elected "Teacher of the Year." I even remember declaring my plans to be like my Mom and get married at 22 to an engineer named John.

And so, suddenly, it was a hot evening in June, and I was in my blue cap and gown, wearing a gold honor-student ribbon and marching down the aisle to receive my diploma. During the picture-taking after the ceremony, I cried as I said goodbye to close friends and well-loved teachers, but underneath it all, I looked forward to college and beyond. It was going to be one exciting life, full of worthwhile accomplishments!

From a high school class of 119, it was quite a step to join 1800 other freshmen on the sprawling campus of Duke University. Right after freshmen week, the upperclassmen returned, and one of the first things they did was look over the new girls and decide who were that year's Duke Duchesses — the ten prettiest freshmen girls. I knew I was just "average," and somehow a "rule of life" established itself in my mind — if you aren't a stand-out in the looks department, the way you get noticed is to work hard and claw your way to the top. So I looked around and found my niche — I'd never be a Big Person on Campus, but I poured everything I had into my major — elementary education. On the social side, I tried to be the basketball team's number one fan.

I loved college life — visiting with friends in the dorm, attending dances and parties, following the basketball team to the NCAA finals. And I was unexpectedly fascinated by geography, art history, and, of all things, a course on Christian marriage. It felt so grown-up, to be talking about weddings and how to handle issues like finances and child rearing.

There were emotional lows, too — taking calculus and never understanding it all semester, waiting in vain for a second call from a blind date I was crazy about, and living through the fear of the Cuban missile crisis. I was sure the world was going to come to an end, before I could even get married. That just didn't seem fair.

Anyway, I was still in one big hurry to get to the next stage of life. Once I met John Preston, a tall, quiet, good-looking junior engineering student, everything seemed to be going perfectly according to my master plan.

Looking back, of course, it is easy to see God's tremendous patience and His protection on my life. I was so firm in my blueprint — my need to find exactly the right man, get married and begin teaching — that I wonder how I would have handled anything else. Fortunately, God smiled and let me do my thing. Soon I was graduating again, and a month later I married my engineer named John. We moved to his hometown, Rochester, New York, where he was already working for Eastman Kodak, and where I began to teach sixth grade. At last, I was on my own — all grown up, with a new husband, a new city, a new job, and a new church.

Everything should have been perfect. It certainly looked good. I loved my teaching job and threw myself totally into it, talking about my "kids" endlessly, morning, noon, and night. Lesson planning was a real challenge, and over all, I felt I was doing a good job and having a positive effect on many young lives. There were inevitably, a few "little" problems: I didn't seem to be able to control the class all the time. Why did they get so noisy when given a little freedom? We often broke up in small groups to do research projects, and it was virtually impossible to keep the noise level down. As a result of raising my voice to get their attention, I often got laryngitis. Evidence of how much it was bothering me on a sub-conscious level, was my recurring "teacher's nightmare" — when I dreamed about a room full of unruly students using bows and shooting arrows at me.

And why was I gaining so much weight? I had begun putting on weight in college, but it seemed to shift into high gear the minute I left the wedding ceremony! John was wonderful, wasn't he? So stable; so secure — but also, so quiet. He would listen to me babble on and on about teaching, but he seldom had much to say about all my great stories and insights. Was it lack of interest? I began to wonder. We had a lovely new house, but we were all alone — the quiet, distracted listener and the constant talker, seeking approval. I had always had a circle of friends to get together with, and missed going out and doing fun things. John, however, was content to stay in the garage, working on his car — a '56 Chevy that he was rebuilding. He loved nothing more than to be out there with that car, surrounded by hundreds of tools. I kept wondering if we should have moved into an apartment, where we could have met other young couples — and where there was no garage.

Following my usual pattern, I plunged ahead to fulfill my goals. Maybe things weren't perfect, but they were pretty good. Most of the time, I was able to gloss over the rough spots, although when my weight gain reached forty pounds, it was hard to ignore. Next on my agenda was a master's degree in education, and I began at the University of Rochester's night school, finishing two years later.

Early in our marriage, we joined Parkminster Presbyterian Church. In spite of my lack of interest in religion, becoming members of a church was something I felt you just did as a matter of course. John agreed with me. Although he was a Methodist, I couldn't imagine myself changing denominations, so we had been trying a different Presbyterian church each Sunday. One afternoon, out of the blue, my father-in-law's former secretary called on me, inviting us to visit her church. That Sunday, we attended Parkminster for the first time — a suburban congregation of several hundred people meeting in a New England style white clapboard building. It was less than two miles from our home and small enough to make it easy to get to know people. The minister was friendly, and his sermons weren't too long. As Goldilocks might have said, "It was just right!"

Once we became members, I expected to be free to attend or not when I felt like it, but here God smiled again: to my surprise, my new husband insisted that we attend every Sunday! All my complaining about the lesson plans I had to do was to no avail. John pointed out that we could go to the early service at 8:30 A.M., and I would have practically the whole day to do homework. So, all of a sudden, quite against my will, I became a regular church-goer again.

After a few Sundays, I got used to it, but I definitely did *not* want to get deeply involved at church. I had not forgotten what had happened to my parents. On the other hand, being a person who didn't like to be left out and who had a terrible time saying "no", gradually I found more and more responsibilities coming my way. Before long, I found myself serving on the Christian Education Committee, running the Junior High Fellowship, and, of all things, doing regular evangelism calling! Me, the non-religious goody-goody!

With all these activities, you may think I had become "born again" or had some kind of religious awakening. No — I was just the same "joiner" I had been in high school. My social life had shifted from a "school" setting to a "church" setting. Since my training was in education, Christian Ed and work with the junior high group seemed like a perfect fit. The evanglism committee was a nice social group and had a great time sharing dinner together once a month. However, a few things did bother me: specifically, some of the junior highs who said they had made "personal commitments to the Lord" and who talked about "Jesus" all the time. They seemed a bit over-excited to me and made me feel uncomfortable. And evangelism calls were okay, as long as a neighborly visit was all that was required. Weren't we just there to invite them to attend church? If anyone had asked a really probing question about God or Jesus, I would have been in deep trouble.

During those years, I had one recurring problem that I couldn't shake: every night when we went to bed, John was out like a light in a minute. No matter how tired I was, I would lay awake for a while — listening. We lived near the airport, so planes passed frequently overhead. From the first tiny engine sound, until it was out of earshot, I held my breath, waiting for the whistling sound of bombs dropping. And these weren't just the old World War II-style bombs, but nuclear bombs which would wipe out the whole city of Rochester. There was no place to hide! I'd never see my parents or brother and sisters again! My life would be blasted away to nothingness! If the sky was quiet, my mind would confront death in another way — I had cancer. I visualized the horrible scene of life going on without me. No one would even care; John would re-marry and love his second wife so much that he'd forget all about me. I wouldn't be remembered. My life was going to end, and I hadn't even done anything yet. I would lay there in terror, with no one to help me until I would finally fall asleep.

As usual, I tried to sweep my concerns under the rug, and had moved on to the next step in my plan: it was time to have a baby and begin our family. Until now, in spite of little ripples, most of my plans had proceeded smoothly. But not now — why do some women get pregnant on the first try? Months dragged by, as we looked for the thrilling symptoms of morning nausea. Eventually we both had to have tests and run our lives by the oh-so-romantic thermometer and temperature charts! It wasn't supposed to be so hard! And it was definitely not in my plan to wait for three years to have a child. Somebody was messing up my plans and I was impatient.

At last, I was eating saltine crackers all day and looking a little pasty-faced — our baby was on the way. I wanted two more children later, and I just knew they would come along in time.

I had to give up teaching, of course, but in the happiness of motherhood, I didn't mind. It was fun being a mother and playing with our little boy, Kirk, and fun to note his progress, as he developed hand-eye coordination. Each day he seemed to be able to do a little bit more.

Kirk was making great progress, but his mother was another story. I had too much free time. You can only spend so long cleaning house and feeding a baby. I had always liked doing crafts and needlework, but that was just a leisure time activity. Gradually, I began to feel useless — and therefore, worthless. For to me, all my worth was tied up in what I could accomplish. Now there were no goals to achieve — no exams to ace, no lesson plans to prepare, nothing . . . I was just a housewife!

The problem was not a lack of things to do; any member of a church knows that there are always plenty of useful ways to invest an available person's time. No, it was more than that; I was caught in the modern woman's dilemma — wanting to be a full-time mother, but feeling of less value than I had when I had been involved in a career out in the world. I found myself volunteering as an aide in the church nursery school — doing now for free what I had been paid to do the year before. I enjoyed the challenge of designing a new playground for the school, but digging twenty-eight post holes for the fence was a drastic change from planning a curriculum.

One morning, sitting alone in the basement, folding diapers, I realized that I had finally come to the end of my blueprint. I had never considered what would happen, when I was no longer working. Nor had I realized the conflict I would face — the struggle between motherhood and a career. My mother and her contemporaries had never worked outside the home, and all my friends had given up their jobs once their children had come along. I had no role model to follow, no plan. Inside, I started to unravel. Ridiculous! I had everything life had to offer! Then why did I feel so — empty?

My weight, which had been stable before the pregnancy, began to rise steadily, going higher than it ever had before. Too much time to sit and think — and be depressed. Too many good things in the kitchen to assuage depression. Too many soap operas to cry along with. Too many rationalizations, too many excuses . . . .

Desperately feeling the need to prove my worth to myself and others, I sought out projects to involve myself in. If I kept busy enough, I might be able to avoid facing what was really going on inside. I decided to single-handedly spring clean the whole church complex. I threw out so much trash that I ended up making brownies to thank the garbage men for hauling it all away, week after week. Another time, I co-chaired a women's luncheon, making crusts and filling for 250 individual pot pies. I made a quilt for my mother and took up freezing and canning fruits and vegetables. I served as chairperson on all kinds of committees.

Yet in the midst of all this activity, I was growing increasingly lonely. Now that I no longer taught school, my social life totally revolved around church. It was a big, alive church, so there was lots to do. But while I knew lots of people there, I had no special close friends. Only much later did I find out I had scared people off, by my drive to accomplish so much. I was so "busy" with all my projects that I didn't have time to stop and be a friend. When I did slow down long enough to talk, I always managed to mention all the things I was doing. What was the use of washing every wall in your house, if no one knows how hard you have been working? So what if I could see that I had made them feel guilty about their own housekeeping — it just proved that I was doing an extra good job.

At home, John was still quiet, and that left Kirk. I talked with him and to him constantly. And John? He generally assumed that it was Kirk I was speaking to, and wouldn't answer me, unless I practically yelled to get his attention.

My emotions went up and down rapidly, and I took everything I felt out on Kirk. I took to calling John "Mr. Perfect," because he did everything so well — in an absolutely disciplined manner. I mean, how could you get angry at someone who exercised regularly, flossed his teeth every day, could fix anything and was happy to do it, and weighed less than he did in high school? So I dumped my pent-up feelings on a defenseless toddler. One minute, I would be playing games and giggling, the next I would be screaming like a maniac. I hated what I saw in myself, but I didn't seem to be able to stop. How had I gotten into such a mess? I might have looked like Wonder Woman to others, but I knew what I was like at home.

What kind of housekeeper was I during this period? Obsessive: besides regular cleaning and spring cleaning, which I got done in February, long before other gals even began thinking about theirs, I worked every day to keep things exactly right. I picked up lint from the rug by hand. I put away every Lego and block just so. I may have been forty pounds overweight, but my house sparkled! And I made a reputation for myself as a consummate hostess — serving elegant, formal, six-course dinners. When company came, everything — even the washing and ironing — was done. Entertaining, decorating and housekeeping were where I shined, so I had to have people over — otherwise, they might just think of me as an overweight, unemployed housewife.

It was at this point that our pastor's wife, Carol Showalter, called to ask me if I wanted to join a new group she was getting together. It was called Diet, Discipline and Discipleship (3D, for short) and was going to be for women who had problems in their lives and needed God's help to work on them. Hating to be left out of anything, I was delighted to have been included in this neat little group, even if I qualified by being one of the heaviest women in the church! About that, I was beginning to have a glimmer of hope. I had seen a few women at church who seemed to really trust God, and believed that He could actually help them. Some people were talking about "Jesus," as if they knew Him personally. A few women who were joining the 3D group were openly admitting that they needed and wanted to be changed. What was going on? I thought that would be the final humiliation: to admit to others how messed up I felt inside.

And so, our little group of ten women began. We kept a diary of what we ate everyday, and weighed in each week. The two leaders guided our weekly discussion time, attempting to help us see what God wanted us to do, and assuring us of His love and care for us. We followed a basic, common-sense diet, and had short teachings from our ministers that helped us to a new perspective on the need for self-discipline. Most significant of all, we prayed for each other — and made a commitment to hold each other in prayer throughout the week.

This business of serious praying was a whole new experience for me. Until then, not counting occasional panic prayers, like when my car would be sliding sideways on an icy expressway bridge (which prayers were probably as much oath as prayer), I hardly prayed at all, even for myself. Most of the twelve-week 3D program, as it was introduced to us, made a lot of sense. But of this one aspect, I was heartily (albeit silently) skeptical. Still, like the others in our group, I had made the commitment, and I was faithful to it. And as I prayed each day, gradually I began to sense a number of things in my heart: I wasn't just talking to my pillow or the steering wheel. He really was *there*. He really *cared*. That broke me up: He *loved* me.

Me, the unloveable — it was a lucky thing for me that I wasn't God; I would have washed my hands of me long ago. But He didn't. He loved me, He listened to my prayers; in fact, He wanted me to pray to Him. And that made me want to, also. I began to look forward to my prayer times, and soon I added John and Kirk to my prayers, and our parents, and other friends, and . . . .

It's a funny thing: when you start praying for someone, your attitude towards them changes; you begin to care in new ways. And it sure takes you out of yourself (at least, while you're praying).

Anyway, what it did for me, where the group was concerned, was to give me the courage to begin to trust. As my relationship with my heavenly Father grew, so did my relationship with the others I was meeting with weekly. I began to understand that God often speaks to one of His children through the lips of another, and that it was true what the Bible said, about Christ being in the midst of a group like ours, which was gathered in His name. I could see Him doing things — Lois was getting her house straightened up, Margaret was losing weight, Sue was finding the strength to face her loneliness. *Alot* of what the Bible said was beginning to make sense on a new, deeper level . . . so much was beginning to happen that my intellect couldn't assimilate it all. No matter, my heart was handling it directly, just fine.

One example of God's love to me in that group was that no one ever pushed me. Week after week, I sat there, taking it all in, never sharing anything. Not once did the leaders put any pressure on me to open up; they seemed to sense that when I felt like it, I would.

And finally, I did. One day, I told the group that that afternoon, I had been hurt about something and had eaten six doughnuts — every last one in the box. They didn't reject me, or even judge me, and I was watching their eyes. They waited to see if I wanted to talk about the hurt. I did, and after that, I had less and less trouble sharing. Because we were all needy, each in our own way, all in the same boat, needing God.

That revelation didn't come all at once; it took time. Eventually, I was even able to talk about the times when I would scream at Kirk. Still no rejection. I began to really care for those women, and I knew they cared for me. What a relief to have a friend to call, when I felt like gulping down a couple of candy bars! What a joy to be able to have a friend over for lunch, who knew me, warts and all. I could be completely honest!

Food, of course, was the part of the program I was having the most difficulty with. Never in my life had I been able to stick to a diet, and this one was no exception. At least my weight gain had finally been stopped. And then one evening, in the middle of one of our meetings, God really put His finger on me.

The meeting was in the chapel of our church — a small, gray-carpeted room, just the right size for our circle of ten chairs. The leaders were looking over our food sheets from the previous week, on which we kept a record of what we ate, and checking them against our weight gains and losses. Again, I hadn't made any progress! My chart didn't look too bad, but as they pointed out, I had made some bad choices each day. I had been easy on myself. Did I really have to have that piece of birthday cake at a friend's party?

Suddenly one of the group members spoke up. She was usually very quiet and shy, but that night she spoke firmly to me. "Why are you in this group?" she asked. "You never follow the diet, and you don't do the things we've all committed to do! You just want to be in the group but you don't want to *do* anything!"

That wasn't true, I thought; I did a lot of the things that we were supposed to, and I used her exaggeration as an excuse to discount what she was saying. She was just angry, because I had cheated on the diet and skipped a few of the other things, and didn't seem to take them seriously.

But for once, I didn't rush to my own defense, insisting that I was doing the best I could. Instead, I nodded and said that I would think about it. I did, and as the meeting went on, I realized that God must have pushed her to say those things, because it was so totally out of character for her. *Was* it you, God, I asked Him — and got convicted that everything she had said was true, and a whole lot more, besides. And then I saw the ultimate truth: I absolutely could not handle my problems on my own; I *needed* Jesus.

Totally out of character, I tearfully told the others what I had just seen. More tears were shed (and not just mine), as I told them that I really would try to trust God, and that with His help, I would be more obedient.

At the end of the meeting, as we stood up to join hands in our prayer circle, I knelt down beside my chair and quietly asked the Lord to take charge of my life. I don't think I spoke aloud, and the others probably didn't know what I was doing. There were no fireworks or angels singing, but I had finally admitted that I couldn't handle my life on my own, and I wanted the Lord to be in charge.

19

Things really began to change after that. With His help, I found I *could* stick to the diet. In fact, it even became fun to lose weight. But what was really exciting, was how He worked in other areas of my life. For He was not just interested in my size; He cared about my loneliness, my fears, my unstable emotions.

The first item on His agenda was teaching me to accept myself as a child of God. This can be a hard lesson to learn. There was no question that I felt better about myself, when my eating was more disciplined. In my group, in Bible reading, in the ministers' teachings, and in my prayer time, I received assurance that God cared for me, fat and angry and all. What a relief! I didn't have to earn His love — He already loved me totally. But could I love myself? Could I make peace with my life, with being a mother and not working outside the home? Amazingly, this huge issue seemed to fade away without me noticing it!

Meanwhile, as I made deep friendships in that group and one that followed it, I became more and more involved in the lives of the people around me. There were so many things to do, caring for and helping others, that it left me little time to worry about where I fit into the scheme of things. I felt fulfilled, as I made coffee cakes for a pre-wedding breakfast a friend was having, or when I helped another friend clean her basement, a friend who really needed help deciding what to keep and what to throw away. One group I was in planned and made a quilt for a newly divorced young mother who was feeling alone and unloved. Another time, we had fun working together to help a couple redecorate their old family homestead.

Eventually I became a 3D group co-leader, where I was called on to care for even more people. I helped them move and clean their houses; I even helped research and write materials for 3D manuals. My life was filled to overflowing. *My* plan had never considered doing what God wanted me to do, let alone doing it for others. But now God had found me, and I had the joy of doing what He gave me to do.

Needless to say, I was never quite the same after that night in the group. I was smaller, for one thing, and a lot more at peace and happy with my life. Gone were the terror-filled dreams and the bursts of anger. And as John began to notice these changes and wonder what had happened to me, lo and behold, a whole new level of communication opened up for us! We joined a couple's sharing group and began a new journey in our marriage — as God took two people who had operated so independently it was as if they were single, and started the long process to make them truly one.

What about my housekeeping? I still like to have things neat and clean, but no longer have the compulsive drive to do it better than anyone else. God has given me so much to do that I no longer have time to make things perfect. I had to learn to adjust my schedule, to care for my home and family, and still have time to be involved with my wider church family. I found I could entertain casually without too much notice, and still do a first-class job; and I could now clean the house in a few hours, instead of several days. I pray about the littlest things now, and gradually, He has given me a whole, new way of looking at bringing His order into my home — and life.

As my involvement with 3D continued, women began asking me to set up home schedules for them. As word of mouth got around, I would be invited to come over and walk through their homes, and make suggestions on how to make the cleaning more manageable. I am still astonished at how well the advice often works — and am reminded that it hasn't come from me. I never set out to have a housekeeping ministry, but it does seem to be a place where God has called on the organizational gift He has given me.

What a joy to see someone else suddenly light up, as if a tremendous burden has been lifted! The guilt of doing a poor job in the home can be heavy, but can He lighten the load! Anyway, I've gathered these experiences into this book, which I pray will be a help.

2

What's the Problem?

So you have your own home! Whether it's an apartment that's too small, or a house that's too big, or just right — now you are trying to take care of it. You may be a full-time homemaker, or you may have a job outside the home, but no matter what, somehow the housework must get done.

No one actually sets out to do a poor job. We mean well — but all kinds of things get in the way. **Time** is often a key problem; there just isn't enough of it. Even the so-called full-time homemaker usually has a number of outside commitments that demand a place in her schedule and make housework hard to finish in the amount of time available.

Children, especially preschoolers, are another problem. Not only do they need your time and attention, and often immediately, but they also seem to *un*do things as fast or faster than you can do them.

On top of everything else, many people lack **self-discipline,** which makes it hard even to get started, let alone do a good job. It's amazing how many really important other things suddenly demand our attention when we get the nudge that we've got to do something about the garage. Or the cabinet under the sink. Or whatever your personal "black hole" is. And then, how hard it is to keep going until the job is finished.

Finally, there's the problem of **lack of knowledge** — of simply not knowing where to start, or what to do.

This book will show you how to schedule your time reasonably, make cleaning your home a manageable task, and still leave you ample time for yourself. What's more, your schedule will be personally tailored to your specific situation and will be flexible enough to change and adjust over the years, to best handle the shifting needs of your family and your other commitments. Sound too good to be true? It isn't; it can be done, and, in fact, is already working for a great many homemakers. Of course, things won't be ever-ready for barracks inspection, but if you learn the general system and make your own adaptations, it definitely is possible to keep your home looking neat and clean.

What is a good housekeeper? We all come to this question with different opinions, which we have picked up through all the people we have known in our lives, especially

23

our mothers. Each of us carries along opinions we have heard from our parents, grandparents, friends, relatives, in-laws, even people we babysat for. Take a moment to step back and look at some of your own life-long ideas.

Maybe your mother, like mine, was considered an excellent housekeeper. How did that affect you? Did you like it and decide to be just like her? Or maybe you thought she went a little overboard, and you'd tone it down just a bit. Possibly she drove you crazy with her neatness and what you saw as an inhuman demand to have everything perfect.

But maybe the opposite was the case. Maybe you were ashamed of how messy she was, and you determined to be meticulous. "I'll never be such a slob! My home will be immaculate!" Or maybe, "I can do better. With a moderate amount of effort, I could keep a home at least decent-looking." Or, "So what's the big deal? We got along fine in a 'casual-looking' home, and so will my family. It's really not worth the hassle."

If your mother fell between the two extremes, you again could have made several different decisions. Maybe you felt pretty good about how she did things and wanted to be just like her. On the other hand, you could have the desire to do a better job than she did — constantly competing with your memories of "how mother did it." Or you might have decided it wasn't really worth the effort; it simply wasn't that important to you. In any event, it is likely that whatever sort of homemaker your mother was, it had a conscious or unconscious effect on how you wanted to be.

Whatever the result, now add to that all the input you bring to homemaking from the whole experience of your life: the gorgeous homes you see in magazines, with fresh flowers in every room; the off-handed comment from your husband about how *his* mother always had dinner on the table at 6:00 and made everything from scratch; the casual remark dropped by a friend about how she spent three hours cleaning her bathroom; the time your grandmother said cleaning a floor didn't count, unless you were down on your hands and knees.

For myself, I remember watching my mother, a fastidious housekeeper, go around on a Sunday afternoon, saying, "This place looks like a pig pen!" I didn't really care that much, and so I decided that I would never do that to my family. I would keep things neat and what I considered "reasonably" clean, but wouldn't overdo it. *I* certainly wouldn't get over-excited, when the Sunday paper was spread all over the family room and things were generally a little out of place.

In short, I had pretty much made up my own mind about how I would keep house, even before I had a house to keep, and long before I learned that I should be listening to Jesus in all things, even that. Although He was there to show me the best way (His way), I wasn't at all ready to pay attention. So I was Humpty-Dumpty — ready to fall. The minute I walked into a room and found it a mess, down I'd go, crashing into a fit of anger. "What do you think I am around here, a slave?" These words were usually spouted off about a mess that five minutes of pick-up could have remedied. Nevertheless, the damage was done; I had dumped my frustrations all over the rest of the family. I had become the kind of wife and mother I never wanted to be.

The problem here was my judgments of my mother and my opinion that I knew the best way to do things. When I was unable to keep things perfectly neat, I would get angry. My anger at myself tumbled out all over whoever happened to be around.

I was also convinced of a number of things about exactly how clean a house must be. I thought I had to wash all the walls every year. I decided this, based on comments I overheard from a person who had a beautiful-looking home. And, of course, everyone knows that you should get on your hands and knees after dinner every day and clean the floor. I saw my mother do it and concluded it was an unwritten rule. (I often skipped it and always felt guilty when I did.) Jesus and I had a lot to work through together, before I could be the woman and homemaker He wanted me to be.

Before you get on with the business of making a realistic schedule and learning how to handle your job as a homemaker, it is important to take time to see where you are coming from. What judgments have *you* made of your mother? What expectations have you already put upon yourself? What opinions have you accepted as truth, without a careful examination? What orders have you consciously or subconsciously given yourself about how you will keep your home? Ask God to help you to be as honest as possible with yourself, in answering these questions:

What did you think of your mother's housekeeping?

What kind of homemaker did you decide you wanted to be?

List some specific ideas you had in your mind that were necessary to be considered a "Good Housekeeper."

What emotions trouble you in relation to your housekeeping? (anger, guilt, competitiveness, etc.)

Are you surprised to see what feelings you have about housekeeping? And where they come from? You asked the Lord to show you your opinions, and He has done it. The next step is to ask His forgiveness for any judgments you may have had, as well as for believing there is only one "right" way to clean a house, your way. If you like, here is a prayer you can use before you go on. (By confessing, you can clean inside, before you clean your house — nothing like getting off to a good start!)

PRAYER: Lord, I confess that I have been in judgment of _____
(Name)
_____. I thought _____
(tell your judgment)
_____. Please forgive me for thinking I know best. I

confess that I have believed there are certain ways a home must be cleaned to be "right." For

instance, I believed _____
(name your opinions)
_____. I accept Your forgiveness and blood washing.

Please change my heart and help me trust You to show me how to clean my house. And Lord,

give me a sense of joy and expectation as I go on with You. Thank You, Lord. Amen.

3

If I Only Had The Time!

Who can find a capable wife? Her worth is far beyond coral. Her husband's whole trust is in her, and children are not lacking . . . She sets about her duties with vigor and braces herself for the work . . . She keeps her eye on the doings of her household and does not eat the bread of idleness . . . it is the God-fearing woman who is honored. Extol her for the fruit of all her toil, and let her labors bring her honor in the city gate. Proverbs 31:1-31 (TEV)

There are so many excuses for not keeping a house in order:
"I could do it, if I only had the time."
"My mother never taught me how."
"I have to do it all alone."
"There are so many more important things to do."

God calls us to care for our homes and our families. He doesn't say do it only if you are a full-time homemaker, or only if you feel like it. Modern conveniences have made it possible for today's woman to hold jobs outside her home, but housework still demands time and effort. Often the way we keep our home reflects what is going on inside of us. A disorderly home can be a sign of rebellion: "God, you are asking too much!"

What you do with your time is a conscious choice. Even though you may feel you are trapped by the demands of your family, your house, and your job, you actually make time-choices constantly. You choose to sit down or to keep moving. You choose to fold clothes or to lay down and watch TV. You chose to put in a load of laundry or to eat a doughnut.

This may be an area where you are having trouble and know you need help. So far, you have taken a look at the ideas you had about cleaning house. You have talked to God about them and asked Him to show you how to proceed. The next step is to **clearly identify your strengths and weaknesses.**

There are many ways to handle housekeeping. Maybe you are totally undisciplined and let things go till the last possible moment, when they absolutely have to be done. Company is coming for supper, and you madly rush around picking up the house and making beds an hour before they arrive.

Or are you the woman who takes on so many outside commitments that she totally neglects her home? There are so many Mission and Outreach meetings that dinner is late every night for a week, and the dishes are still piled by the sink at bedtime.

Maybe you work hard at home but never feel done — rarely having time for things you "want" to do, or for relaxation. The house is in good condition, but you haven't sat down to play the piano or done any sewing for months.

Some people find they flit around the house from job to job never finishing anything. Others feel they do some housekeeping jobs quite well, but are terrible at others. Maybe you keep things up well from week to week, but don't get to deep ("spring") cleaning. You may work hard but don't ever feel good about what you have done.

How would you describe your style of house cleaning?

Right now, you need to prayerfully consider in detail, how you clean house. Look at each of the items below and check the appropriate boxes:

	Things I like to do	Things I don't like to do	Things I do well	Things I neglect	Things I need help to learn
Daily pick-up					
Weekly cleaning bathrooms					
bedrooms					
kitchen					
living-dining					
family room					
"Spring" cleaning storage area					
walls					
windows					
floors, rugs					
redecorating					
Grocery shopping					
Laundry					
Wardrobe up-dating					
Finances					
Sewing					
Meal Preparation					
Yard work					
Special projects					
Hobbies					
Helping others					
Relaxation					
Quiet time with Jesus					
Personal Hygiene					
Exercise					

Now you have faced where you are, with all its blemishes and beauty marks. There is definitely room for improvement. Trust the Lord. He knows what you should do and how much time you have to do it. Each of these concerns will need to be considered, as you make your schedule later in the book.

4

What Does Clean Mean?

What does *clean* mean, to you and to the other members of your household? No two people agree totally. But before you can dig in and get that housework done, you need to see clearly what your goals are. What bothers you the most? What specifics make you feel that the house is messy? Identifying the trouble spots is the first step to wiping them out.

Think about how you feel, as you walk around your house. What are the things that make you mutter under your breath — "Oh, no, not again! Doesn't anyone else care about this house at all?" What little jobs do you feel you do and re-do fifty times a week?

I used to just "love" coming home from a Monday evening Christian Education meeting to find everyone had gone to bed, leaving *Sports Illustrated* or *Time* or the paper dropped on the floor by the couch and empty ice cream bowls on the end table and the top of the TV. It seemed that every time I passed the bathroom some "mysterious" person had left the toilet seat up. It was just a reflex movement to put it down and grumble. My husband used to get annoyed when the dish drainer was piled high with clean dishes. "Why can't these be dried and put away? It would only take a few minutes," he would complain, coming home from a late Session meeting. And then he would do them himself. Neither of us liked to see the kitchen wastebasket stuffed so full that the lid was sticking up. And then there was an empty gallon milk jug, or a discarded cereal box left over from an after school snack.

What bothers you? Sit down with the people you live with, to see what they think. See what changes you can all institute, to make all of you feel more comfortable about how the house looks. Often you will find it's the little things — the open closet doors and cluttered kitchen counters — rather than big things, like dirty windows or soiled rugs. Draw up a list together; it will give you a clear picture of where to begin your cleaning.

31

What things bother you and make you feel your house is messy or out of order?

What things bother others in the home (spouse, roommate, children, etc.)?

And when things are not always kept the way that you've agreed (and they won't be; nobody's perfect — not even you), try to keep your cool. Many times the devil manages to upset us simply by pointing out these little annoyances. He knows how to get us down. "Ah ha," he gloats, "I know Mary Jane hates seeing the bath mat crooked and the shower curtain left open, so that the dirty tub shows. And it drives her crazy when the closet door is shut with a coat sticking out." We shouldn't let him beat us so easily.

After many years of being bothered when things around the house weren't straightened up my way, I finally stepped back and thought about my alternatives. I decided I have four possible plans of attack:

1. I can give it up. The following example may sound petty, but I suspect we all have such little idiosyncracies. I like the bath mat folded in half, with the fold hanging on the inside of the tub and the corners on the outside. Of course, I want the corners to meet evenly and hang down straight. It seemed that no matter how many times I hung or rehung it that way, everyone else put the fold on the outside of the tub. So I decided, why buck traffic; it didn't matter. Now I hang it my way, but when it's the other way, that's okay. Why waste energy over such a trifle?

And talk about trifles, could anything be more ridiculous than arguing about which way the toilet paper should face? Believe it or not, newspaper columns have been devoted to this subject, eliciting vehement letters to the editor! What earthly difference does it make? (It certainly doesn't make any heavenly difference.) What *does* matter are those who would leave two squares of paper on the end of the roll, so that technically they won't have to be the one to replace it. That is *verboten*. (But just in case, it is not a bad idea to keep a reserve roll near by.)

2. I can do it myself. I have tried to teach my children that a room looks neater when closet doors are shut, however, they often don't quite get them closed all the way. So, since it bothers me, I just close them as I move around the house. If they've made their beds neatly and hung up their clothes, and done all the other things their father and I insist on, is it worth calling them back to shut a door? I've decided it's not. But since I personally prefer it closed, I do it myself.

3. I can enlist the help of the family. Back in the bathroom again, we have a shower curtain problem. Since we now have a large family and only one tub, it sees frequent use. If the curtain is always left at one end, it eventually gets moldy inside the folds. Besides that, I like it pulled closed, in case the tub is not exactly gleaming, and I think our shower curtain is really attractive. For a long while, I felt like I was the only one who left it pulled. I finally decided it was worth the time and effort to explain it to each family member, one by one, and ask them to help. Since then, I rarely have to fix it. When I told them why I cared about it, they were willing to do it my way.

4. I can assign it to someone else. The over-stuffed kitchen wastebasket constantly sneaks up on me, so I assigned it to Kirk. It's now his responsibility to notice when it is filling up, and if I happen to be the one to see it, I call on him to empty it.

List the things that bother you under Annoyance, and then the number of the way you will handle each one: 1. give it up; 2. do it yourself; 3. enlist the whole family; 4. assign a family member.

Annoyance   **Plan of Attack**

There are bigger issues to be decided too, of course. Family members set different priorities. You may hate clutter and spend a lot of time, straightening things. On the other hand, your spouse may care much more about what time dinner is served, preferring to have a regular time that he can plan his commitments around. Or maybe he usually has an early lunch, and is famished by 6:30 P.M. In many homes, laundry is a real bone of contention — poor husbands left with no clean shirts to wear, or children who can't get dressed because all of their underwear is in the washer.

Are you in agreement about redecorating and repair projects? You may want the family room rug replaced as soon as possible, because the worn spots are driving you crazy. Your husband, however, may have re-doing the downstairs bathroom as his top priority. He hates the pink fixtures. Whatever you do, discuss your concerns thoroughly before rushing to make any changes.

What issues cause conflict?

Use the space below to write the problems and the solutions you agree upon. Two examples:

Conflict	Solution
1. Spouse and children nag me, if dinner is ready after 6:30 P.M.	1. Plan to serve dinner regularly at 6:15 P.M. Check early in day, to see when I will need to start cooking the meal.
2. I want to redecorate the girls' bedroom. John says we can't afford it.	2. We agree to consider a total re-doing of the bedroom when he gets his annual bonus next year. For now, we can buy new comforters for the beds and matching curtains.

Now, your turn:

Conflict	Solution

(continued)

Conflict	Solution

Once you have talked things out, you will have a realistic picture of what you are trying to accomplish. It all may seem to be an impossible task, but by the grace of God, you can do it. You won't be able to keep up with everything all the time, but God knows what needs to be done. And He really will assign top priority, if you will ask Him. The key is to keep your lines of communication open. Ask Him what to do next. Let Him direct you.

Here are some simple routines which can help you keep up with your housework. Pray and see which of these might work for you. But if you decide to do one or more, really make up your mind to stick with it every day.

Morning Pick-Up   If you have to leave the house at a certain time each morning, plan to set aside ten or fifteen minutes for a walk-through of the house, doing a quick pick-up and general straightening. It will give you a good feeling when you leave — and make it easier, when you come home.

Afternoon Pick-Up   Maybe it makes more sense for you to have a general pick-up just before diner. This is especially true if you have preschoolers. Then, when you sit down to your meal, you won't be discouraged by all the work left to do after dinner.

Bedtime Pick-Up   On your way up to bed is another time you might choose to spend ten minutes straightening up. Maybe you are better at night than you are in the morning. It can be depressing to wake up to a messy house. You are behind, before your day even begins. Pick the time that best suits your personality, your family and your schedule.

Serve breakfast   If you have an especially hard time getting started in the morning, it might help if you disciplined yourself to serve your family a simple breakfast. One woman I know said this could never work for her. Her morning mood was so negative that her husband told her she was a grouch, and he'd rather she'd stay in bed. After praying, she decided to try it anyway. When I saw her a week later, her face was shining. Wonder of wonders, her husband loved having her fix him a little breakfast! She said that just doing that each day had changed eveyrthing. She felt like a whole new thing was happening in her marriage. And children appreciate the same disciplined care.

Put Away the Dishes   If dishes in the dishwasher or drainer bother you or your husband, then make plans to get them put away. Decide to do it regularly yourself, or assign it to other family members on a rotating basis. If you make plans to handle a problem, you will feel much better.

Dinner on Time   Lack of discipline about when dinner is served is one of the most frequent causes of conflict or bad feelings. Agree on the best time and then really work at sticking to it. Just this simple thing will give structure to the entire day. Everyone will know when to be home, the kids won't have to keep nagging you to ask "When is dinner?", and you will know how much time you have left for your evening commitments.

Check which daily goals you plan to include in your schedule to help you keep up with your housework:

_____ Morning pick-up

_____ Afternoon pick-up

_____ Bedtime pick-up

_____ Serve breakfast

_____ Put away dishes

_____ Dinner on time

5

Everything in its Place

This is the *key* to getting your house in order. Unless things have certain places where they belong, the house will never really look clean. Conversely, when things are in their places, a house will look well, even when it isn't totally clean.

When you moved into your home, you enjoyed settling in. Furniture was arranged, drawers and closets were filled. You indulged yourself in "nesting." Now, a few months (or years) later, the place always looks messy, and you wonder why you loved the house or apartment so much, or thought that it was just the right size for you. Time has passed and not only are things out of place, but many new items have been added — none of which really has its own special "home."

This problem is especially noticeable after Christmas, when it's time to put away all the gifts. The new toy garage with ten cars won't fit on the toy shelves in your son's bedroom. How can you squeeze your daughter's new stereo into her room? What about your husband's weights and bar bells, and your wok? Should you shove the weights under the bed? Can you fit the wok on top of the refrigerator, next to the bowl of fruit and yesterday's newspaper? If you put the stereo in the corner on a little plastic table, where will all her records go? "Well, I'm in a rush right now," you think. "I'll just stick it the first place I can find."

It may seem too easy, but **Establishing a Place Where Each Thing Belongs** is a key to having a neat home. The house will never look picked up, unless you have somewhere to put things once you have picked them up. What good does it do to gather up all the newspapers and magazines, if you end up piling them in a corner beside the couch? What good does it do to tell your kids to clean up their rooms, if they have so many things crammed into the room that it looks messy even when they have finished?

Once or twice a year, take time to go through your home and establish where things belong. The first time it will be a big job, but once you get into the habit, you will be able to do it quickly.

The most important thing is to step back and see how the house looks. Where are the problem spots? What items keep getting in the way? You may have switched from using a curling brush to a blow dryer. Because both appliances have been left on the same shelf, the cords get tangled up, and when you reach for the dryer, you get the brush, too. It makes sense to store the curling brush somewhere less accessible, so the item you really need is easy to reach.

Are there things you are using more often and need to have in a handier place? Maybe you have decided you like a pitcher of water on the kitchen table at dinner. If so, wouldn't it be a good idea to find a *convenient* storage space, instead of in the bottom compartment of the china cupboard on the other side of the dining room?

Other things that are used less frequently now don't require the most accessible storage. That bin of wooden blocks your pre-schooler once played with every day is now used only occasionally. A spot in the basement would probably be better than the prime location in the family room which it currently occupies.

Maybe you need new shelves or racks or hooks or containers, in order to store items neatly and handily. Use catalogs and look in stores to get ideas of what would work well for you. I know a friend whose garage looked like ground zero after a bombing raid. Her husband finally put shelves on every wall that would hold them, except for where he put a pegboard to hang garden tools. And he was so carried away with enthusiasm when he finished, that he doubled the size of her food storage shelves in the basement. That meant she could make one less food-shopping trip a week. The garage can still get messy, but it can also look astonishingly neat.

Storage decisions may be simple or creative. A plastic dish pan is handy for cereal boxes or loaves of bread or cleaning supplies and can be easily pushed into a cabinet. A fishing tackle box works well for those hundreds of Lego pieces. It can also make an excellent repository for household tools, and all those odd screws and "attachers" that you can't bring yourself to throw out, as well as those wierd bits of electrical stuff that wind up in the kitchen "junk drawer."

When my mother made me a gorgeous fisherman's knit afghan, I wanted it to be visible but not just laying around. A perfect solution was a pine towel rack on the family room wall. A new meat platter may call for a special plastic rack of its own, suspended under a wooden shelf inside a cabinet. Your daughter's doll clothes could be stored in a small set of cardboard drawers inside her closet.

Besides these, you can also use:
— plastic wastebaskets for sets of toys
— baskets for yarn or embroidery floss
— boxes attractively covered with contact paper for gift wrapping supplies
— steel, wrought iron, or wooden shelves for boots and rubbers in winter months
— a hanging bag with pockets for shoes to hold mittens, scarves, and caps

Once each item has an established place, your weekly and daily cleaning will go much more smoothly. The children will know where to put things when they clean up, and so will you. With less stuff laying around, there will be less for you to clean. And don't try to use the excuse that leaving something out (a sewing project, letter-writing paraphernalia, piles of bills, etc.) will help you get the job done faster. It will make you feel guilty each time you glance at it, but will rarely make you do it sooner.

For instance, where will you keep the material, pattern, and notions for your new dress? In the basement where I sew, I use a deep carboard box lid on a storage shelf. Anytime I am ready to sew, I slide the lid out and put it on the table where I work. If I leave it on the table all the time, besides inducing guilt, it takes up the space where I fold clothes and where I do other craft projects.

Evaluating your storage problems and needs will become a part of your regular once or twice a year "Big Cleaning."

What clutters up your home? (no established place)	Where should it go?	Does it require purchasing any hardware or storage items?

What clutters up your home? (no established place)	Where should it go?	Does it require purchasing any hardware or storage items?

6

Setting Up A Flexible Schedule

Now it's time for you to take your first big step: setting up a flexible schedule. This will provide the basic framework you need to move confidently through your week.

If you have children, you know that, while they will probably not admit it, they really desire some discipline and orderliness to their days. Take away that structure from their activities — go shopping all day and eat two hours late — and before you know it, you will have a very cranky child on your hands. Adults are often the same way. A whole afternoon lies ahead of you. Think of all you can do in that block of free time. Then suddenly, four hours have gone by, and besides a two-hour nap, watching a little TV, and carrying a few things to the basement, you realize you have accomplished little. Then the kids wonder why a very touchy mother is banging around the kitchen, angrily making dinner.

It seems that for years we strive to grow up, to become independent. Now finally we can do what we want, when we want to do it! But in throwing discipline out of our lives, we lose more than we bargained for. We are "free" — but at what a price!

Although it may take a while for you to really believe it, the truth is that if you work by a schedule, you will get more done and feel better about your life — and will still have time to do things you want to do. Your schedule should be a realistic goal — sufficient time set aside to accomplish necessary tasks.

Fill in a Calendar for a Month

The first step is to help yourself get a clear picture of your present commitments. Fill in a calendar for the next four weeks. List hours you work, commitments that involve your children, and meetings, classes, parties, and other events you plan to attend.

Use the blank calendar in Appendix A to fill in your activities for the next four weeks.

Here is a sample calendar, already filled in. It gives an idea of what a month in my life is like.

Sunday	Monday	Tuesday	Wednesday	Thursday	Friday	Saturday
Church 9-12 Sledding party 2-5	Work Tutor 12:30-3:30 Bell Choir 6:30 Meeting 7:30	8:30-12 noon	Tutor 12:30-3:30	Meeting 7:30-10:30	Basketball Game 7:00	10-2 Basketball Game
Church 9-12	Work Tutor 12:30-3:30 Bell Choir 6:30	8:30-12 noon	Tutor 12:30-3:30 6-8 Dinner with Friends		5-12 Take Kids Skiing	8:00 Party
Meeting 7:30-10:30	Work Tutor 12:30-3:30 Bell Choir 6:30	8:30-12 noon	Tutor 12:30-3:30	2:30 Haircut Meeting 7:30		11-2 Meeting
Church 9-12 Family Night @ Church 5-8	Work Tutor 12:30-3:30 Bell Choir 6:30	8:30-12 noon	Tutor 12:30-3:30		9:00 Movie	
Church 9-12 Meeting 7:30-10:30	Work Tutor 12:30-3:30 Bell Choir 6:30	8:30-12 noon 7:30 Open House	6-8 Dinner with Friends			

Consider the Tasks

As the primary person responsible for the upkeep of the home, there are numerous tasks which you will need to accomplish, including:

> grocery shopping
> laundry — washing, folding, ironing
> regular weekly housecleaning
> meal preparation
> occasional heavy (spring) cleaning

Beyond those are other jobs which someone will need to be responsible for:
> finances
> yard work
> wardrobe shopping
> car maintenance
> household repairs

And don't forget the things you *want* to do:
> hobbies
> special projects
> sewing
> letter writing
> reading
> personal hygiene
> exercise

Consider the Implications

Before you can actually fill in your own weekly schedule, you need to step back and look at your life. You have made choices about your involvements, but perhaps not from the perspective that every choice affects how much time you have left to fulfill your duties at home. Have you talked to the Lord about your decisions? If not, you should spend a few minutes reviewing your outside commitments with Him.

Do you need to work outside the home? Consider this carefully: are you willing and able to handle having this large chunk of your day spoken for? Is this the best choice for you? For your family? If the answer is "Yes," then you need to be realistic when you look at the rest of your schedule. Don't try to be Wonder Woman!

Who else can help with the chores? Can the children take on some responsibilities? (A later chapter will help you see how to get them involved in working around the house.) Will you hire someone regularly or occasionally? Will your spouse or roommate work with you to get things done? Depending on their talents, interests, and time, they can decide what their contributions will be. For example, my husband handles all the car maintenance and most household repairs. A few years ago, he took over doing the monthly bills — a change which took a great load off my mind. Lawn mowing and lawn care take some of his attention in the summer; I handle the gardens and leaf raking. John feels it is important for him to help our daughter Joy with her homework, so this is a job we share.

Are you overcommited? Will you need to cut down on commitments beyond your home and job to make things more manageable? If so, what should you drop? Some things may be easy to let go, but I usually find it difficult to give up things I am involved in. This is definitely a matter for prayer. As you talk with the Lord, tell Him the facts — all that is on your schedule, what you enjoy, what you dislike, what you feel called to. Trust Him to help you figure out what you should do in the available time.

It is helpful to to talk over these concerns with someone else — your spouse, or a close Christian friend. They can often see your situation more clearly than you can yourself. Once you have settled these issues, you should be able to list the chores that will be your responsibilities.

My Responsibilities

Setting Up Your Weekly Schedule

The key now is to mesh together your outside commitments and your at-home responsibilities. On the next page is a schedule similar to one I have made out for myself:

Time	Sunday	Monday	Tuesday	Wednesday	Thursday	Friday	Saturday
5:50-6:15		Mile Walk	→	→	→	→	
6:15-7:30	7:30 Breakfast	Make Breakfast, Pack Lunches, Make bed, Quick House Straightening*	→	→	→	→	
7:30-7:45		Quiet Time	→	→	→	→	
7:45-8:15	8:00 Personal Hygiene	Personal Hygiene — Bath, Make-up, Hair, Dress	→	→	→	→	
	CHURCH			WORK		Strip Beds	9-12 noon Regular Weekly Housecleaning
		TUTORING	1-2 Laundry / 2:00-3:30 Big Job or Special Project	1-3 Grocery Shopping	TUTORING	1-3 Laundry	1-5 Hobby or Big Job or Special Project
12-2	Lunch Read Paper						
2-6	Hobby or Sewing or Letterwriting or Relaxation						
3:30-5:00		Odd Jobs around House and Time with Kids and Errands	→	→			
5:00-7:00		Dinner Preparation and Serving and Clean up	→	→			
		BELL CHOIR	Make Menu and Shopping List	DINNER WITH FRIENDS		Remake Beds	
10:15-10:30	Personal Hygiene	☆	☆	☆	☆	☆	☆

* Kids do dishes, make beds, empty wastebaskets, get dressed, pick up bedrooms.

☆ If no meeting takes up this time — do odd jobs, special projects, sew, read, relax, ironing

1. Daily Jobs: Set aside time for everyday jobs:

Daily Jobs	Time
— making beds	_____
— straightening up	_____
— dinner preparation	_____
— quiet time	_____
— help children with homework	_____
— making bag lunches	_____
— personal hygiene	_____

2. Weekly Jobs: After carefully considering your present commitments, set up blocks of time for doing weekly tasks:

Weekly Jobs (Pencil these in because you may need to change them periodically.)	Time
— laundry	_____
— stripping beds	_____
— changing bathroom linens	_____
— regular weekly cleaning	_____
— ironing	_____
— menu planning and grocery shopping	_____
— re-making beds	_____

3. Yearly Jobs and Special Projects: Although certain jobs need to be done only once a year (i.e. washing walls) time needs to be reserved. Each week, tentatively schedule several blocks of time for big jobs and special projects. What you will actually do then will vary from month to month.

— window washing	_____
— "spring" cleaning	_____
— sewing	_____
— shopping	_____
— yard work	_____
— redecorating	_____

4. Personal Time: Besides all these things which must be done are the things you like to do. We all need time to relax, to do something we enjoy. Your schedule should include blocks of time set aside for yourself — times to read, times to write, times to be creative, times to take a deep breath and be refreshed.

Now you are ready to set up your own weekly schedule. Use the blank calendar and step-by-step directions in Appendix B. Pray as you work on it. Ask the Lord to show you what to include. Don't try to make yourself "instantly perfect," but include only as much as He directs.

Once you feel comfortable with the way you have constructed your schedule, make a copy of it and keep it posted in a handy spot at home. You can begin using it right away. As you read in this book, you will be learning how to get more done in a shorter period of time, but even without these refinements, your schedule can be a big help.

Learn to Bend and Adjust

Remember — there are two key words: flexible and schedule. The schedule is to give you a sense of structure and direction. People seem to operate best within some kind of a general framework for their time. Once you have made yourself a schedule, use it. Don't disregard it too readily. Don't say "yes" everytime you are asked to do something by family or friends. Think carefully and pray, before you chuck your plans out the window. Don't take on so much that your family and your home suffer.

But be flexible. The schedule is to help you, not tie you in knots. Don't be legalistic. When special events disrupt your usual weekly calendar, bend and adjust. When Saturday morning is the time your son has a basketball game, move your cleaning to the afternoon. If there is no time Wednesday evening for making your grocery list, do it that afternoon or during lunchtime on Thursday. And as things have to be switched around or, even skipped for one week — relax. The world won't end, if you don't wash the sheets every seven days.

Look back, for a moment, over the past month. What kind of interruptions did you have? A child coming down with chicken pox is good for lots of schedule-juggling. Maybe your sister's family stopped overnight on their way to Florida, or someone dropped over to borrow a special cake pan and stayed to talk all evening. You planned to go grocery shopping but ended up going to the hospital with a friend who had an ultrasound exam. Whether you realized it or not, you adjusted your plans to accommodate the changes. Your family still ate dinner, and somehow the laundry did get done.

A written schedule helps you to know exactly what responsibilities need re-arranging. If your evening with a friend wiped out the time you had planned to clean some closets, look to see when you can reschedule it. Staying home with a sick child will mean a switch for your grocery shopping. Maybe you can do it in the evening, when your husband is home. In the meantime, the afternoon can be put to good use tackling the sewing project you had planned to do after supper.

When something new appears on your calendar, take a few minutes to think. Does the change mean you will need to move things around on your schedule? Or does it mean something will need to be dropped this week? If you can make a realistic decision, you won't find yourself staying up late, madly trying to squeeze too many things into one day. The important thing is to *think* and decide, rather than merely being tossed about by the winds of change.

7

Big Cleaning

Now that you have made a schedule and have looked for the problem areas in your housekeeping, you are ready to clean. When people talk about cleaning, they are generally referring to "weekly" chores. One of the purposes of this workbook is to help you get these weekly jobs down to a manageable level, so that the house will look nice, and you will still have time for your family and outside commitments.

A key to making weekly cleaning quick and easy is to do a **Big Cleaning** of your home, once or preferably twice a year. This keeps things basically clean, and clutter weeded out, so that your regular chores are mostly surface — straightening, pick-up, and touch-up.

In your schedule you have set aside time for special projects. These will vary with the time of year — gardening, raking leaves, Christmas shopping and decorating, and window washing, for example. Twice a year, use this time to do a Big Cleaning.

1. Select the months to do your Big Cleaning

Take a look at the flow of your year and pick two months approximately half a year apart, when you will spend some of your special project time on this "spring" cleaning.

Years ago, I chose January and July. January was usually a quiet month, and there were all those gifts from Christmas to put away — a good time to tackle storage problems. July was about half a year away and worked well for me when I was teaching, as it fell between the end of school in June and going on vacation in August. Now that I work at a year-round job, I find these months continue to work well. January is still a less busy month. In July I am a little freer and the kids are available to "big clean" their own rooms. If I need to hire someone to help me, lots of teenagers are around and anxious to make a little money. I tend to be more thorough, hitting more of the big jobs in the winter. It is snowy and cold in Rochester, and I don't ski! I try to stagger the hardest jobs — maybe washing walls in January and shampooing the rugs in July.

2. Make a list of proposed jobs

Actually go from room to room with a pen and notebook. List what needs to be done in each room. Also note things you would like to do, if finanaces and time permit. Consider these four concerns:

— Storage
   Cleaning drawers, cupboards, closets, and shelves; making decisions on where things belong; purchasing and installing new storage devices.
— Heavy Cleaning
   Washing walls, vacuuming with attachments to get everywhere, shampooing carpets, cleaning upholstery, washing all knick-knacks, stripping and waxing floors
— Special Projects
   Making repairs, replacing worn out items, mending
— Re-decorating
   Painting, wallpapering, re-upholstering, new furniture or curtains, new decorative touches, re-arranging furniture.

Here is how I would evaluate my living room and dining room. I would start my list with cleaning drawers and the inside of the china cupboard. Silver needs to be polished. I painted the walls last year, and they don't need washing yet, however the molding trim needs to be cleaned. The rugs are all right, except for the edge by the hall which I plan to scrub. The couch, chair, and rug edges need careful vacuuming. The vases, china pieces and tray which are decorative objects need to be washed. As far as repairs go, a little piece of wallpaper is ripped at one corner and needs to be re-glued. The finishes of the top of the cherry end tables and dining table have progressivley been getting more smeared-looking. I write down a reminder to call the manufacturer.

Upon checking, I learn I had been using a spray polish and should have been using lemon oil. Now I have to wash them with oil soap and rub them down with lemon oil and 0000 steel wool. That will be the one big job to tackle in that room. No redecorating will be needed for several years until the rug needs replacing. If we have the money next winter, I would like to have our good sofa professionally cleaned.

Based on all the above information, here is the list I would write down for "Big Cleaning" the living room, dining room area:
   — all storage — clean and straighten
   — polish silver
   — vacuum — rug, sofa, chair, drapes
   — shampoo carpet edge by door to hall
   — clean knick knacks
   — re-glue torn wallpaper
   — rub down top of tables
   — dust all furniture thoroughly, top to bottom

— clean off molding trim around bottom of room

— check plants to see if any need replacement or repotting

— consider having professionals clean sofa next winter

You may wonder why I would note something for next winter, as I moved from room to room. Later I will turn to the page on my calendar for next January and jot down "blue couch cleaned." This way, I don't have to think about it for six months. In January, I will see my note, and John and I will decide whether we can afford it. This eliminates having all kinds of little nagging feelings about things that need doing around the house. I have written them down for a time when I plan to consider action. It saves lots of worry and vague dissatisfaction. I can relax; I have made plans.

All kinds of odds and ends show up on my room-cleaning lists. I include everything in the room, so in the kitchen I make a note to update my recipe file with all the recipes I have collected over the past six months. In the front hall closet, where we store slide trays, I remember to put the recent slides in their slots and label them. The family room lamp shades need replacing and a wall wreath needs more babies' breath added to it (the cat keeps pulling it out!). I need to paint the insides of the bathroom cupboards and buy a new shower curtain. Because I have begun buying canned goods by the case (we joined a food co-op), I need to re-arrange part of a cupboard in the basement to accommodate them. When I clean my desk drawers, the baby books for the children need to have comments written in them for what they have been up to recently. In short, the lists are a great place to jot down all the jobs it is so easy to forget.

3. Schedule your cleaning

Once your room lists are made, take a look at your calendar for the coming months and see how you can schedule your Big Cleaning. I usually begin at the "top" of the house with the bedrooms and work my way down to the basement. That way, as I do each room, I can take things we no longer need downstairs. Then when I clean the basement, I box these items up for a summer garage sale or give them away.

If you have two time periods a week for special projects, you can schedule one or two rooms for cleaning. Tentatively pencil in the names of which room you will tackle on the days on your calendar.

For instance, your schedule might look like this:

Week 1: 2 bedrooms
Week 2: 1 bedroom / 2 bathrooms
Week 3: hall / kitchen
Week 4: living room / family room
Week 5: basement

4. Do repairs

Before you get down to cleaning a room, take time to make minor repairs. Re-glue the torn wallpaper, fix the hole that the door stopper made in the door, replace the splintered piece of edge trim molding, replace the broken window shade. Now is the time to correct all the little problems that annoy you about the room. Purchase new lamp shades, if the old ones are soiled and can't be washed. Buy a new wastebasket to replace a beat up one. Tighten the screws on the drawer pulls. Replace the loose picture hook or re-hang the curtain rod more securely. Call an upholsterer and have the popped button on the couch replaced.

5. Redecorate

A room that is going to be redecorated needs extra time and effort. So, make your plans and schedule accordingly. Are you going to do it yourself or hire help? If you are doing it, don't plan to do a lot of other big jobs in other rooms at almost the same time. Be realisitc and don't overschedule yourself. Once the painting and/or papering are done, you will go on to do cleaning.

6. Clean

The time has come to dig in and do a specific room. Where do you start? Use your list of proposed jobs as a guide and begin with storage.

Go through each closet and drawer — cleaning and straightening it. Make decisions as you go along. Re-arrange things to make them more convenient. And don't be afraid to throw things away! If you have a hard time getting rid of things, have a place in the basement or garage where you can put them. Then set a later deadline for yourself, to go through these stored items and make final decisions.

Once the clutter is removed, you are ready to do heavy cleaning. Start at the top of the room and work down:

— **Dust or vacuum ceiling** for cobwebs

— **Wash walls,** if necessary. If walls are heavily soiled, use a liquid cleaner. For normal to light soil, I use a spray glass cleaner or a spray foam bathroom cleaner and wipe with old towels. Problem spots require products such as "Fantastic" or "409."

— **Clean knick-knacks.** I use glass cleaner on picture frames and glass over pictures. Pieces of china, glass lamp shades and the like can be washed in soapy water, rinsed and dried. Artificial flower arrangements may be dusted off or rinsed to brighten the petals.

— **Vacuum drapes and upholstered pieces**

— **Wash or dry clean curtains,** if necessary. Frequency depends on how they look and the traffic in the area. Kitchen curtains need to be done more often than those in the bedrooms. Good drapes shouldn't be cleaned too often, but may need to be vacuumed with a soft, clean brush attachment.

— **Clean pieces of furniture and appliances.** For wood pieces this usually means a thorough dusting of all surfaces. Occasionally you may need to wash with soap and water and follow with a new coat of polish. Follow the directions of the manufacturer, and if you don't have these, call a store that sells them. Another information source is your local home extension bureau. Do the appliances with a glass cleaner. Of course, when you are doing the kitchen, this involves a complete cleaning of the refrigerator and stove, inside and out — and behind and under — vacuuming coils, using oven cleaner, washing drawers and racks.

— **Do the floor or rug.** Assess how much cleaning is needed. The floor may only need a washing, or it might require washing and a new coat of surface protector; possibly it may need to be stripped and waxed. Again, make sure you are using the correct products, according to the manufacturer. Call the store if you are unsure. The rug may need only a thorough vacuuming using edge tools and moving the furniture to get everywhere. There may be a few spots that need a spray rug cleanser and scrubbing with a brush. If a complete shampooing is called for, you can rent a machine or hire someone else to do it. But if you are bringing home a machine, be sure to consider doing several rooms at once. For instance, you can clean all the bedrooms and then rent a cleaner and do all these carpets at once.

7. Reschedule as necessary, but keep going until all the rooms are done.

If you don't get to a room, or if you aren't able to complete the area according to your schedule, move it to your next block of time for special projects. This will necessitate moving all the rooms along on your calendar. Keep working towards completing the house. Don't feel guilty! You are working on the job and you intend to complete it.

Ask the Lord to guide you. Sometimes it is hard to keep at the jobs; other times, it is difficult to stop and do regular tasks or spend time with your children. The Lord knows your excuses, and will help you to see them for what they are: work-avoidance techniques. He also knows how to curb your drive to be perfect. Let Him be in control of your schedule. Talk to Him each day about your plans, listen for His direction, and heed it.

It is a great feeling to complete your list, to know the house has truly been cared for and is basically, deep-down clean. Now the upkeep from week to week will be so much easier.

I plan to do my Big Cleaning in: (circle two months)

JAN   FEB   MAR   APR   MAY   JUN   JUL   AUG   SEPT   OCT   NOV   DEC

Here is space to do your room-by-room list of proposed jobs. Be realistic; this first time you will probably need to spend extra time on cleaning storage areas, so don't overcommit yourself to heavy cleaning all the rugs, walls or curtains.

Master Bedroom

Bedroom

Bedroom

Bathrooms (do them as a group)

Halls & Stairways

Living room

Dining room

Kitchen

Family room

Study (or other room)

Basement

Garage

Others:

8

Weekly Cleaning

Most families enjoy having their home neat and clean, although it is a place where they should also be able to relax. Weekly cleaning is the commitment required to keep things up-to-date, picked up, straightened up, dusted, vacuumed and shined up.

Once you have done your "Big Cleaning," the weekly jobs will go much more quickly, but even if you have not done the deep cleaning yet, you can still keep things in shape on a week-to-week basis. For heaven's sake, don't attempt to spring clean every room every seven days! Only plan to do what really needs to be done weekly. Dusting, yes; vacuuming under the couch, no.

What time have you set aside on your calendar? A morning, a day, an afternoon, two mornings? If you are home much of the time, or have children at home all day, you may need to clean more, due to more traffic. The time you need to set aside will vary over the years, as will the time slot you select. I usually re-evaluate my schedule at the beginning of each school year. When I was home with my children, I usually cleaned on Friday — half a day or a whole day, depending on my availability. At another time, I did it Thursday and Friday afternoons during their naps — doing the upstairs one day and the downstairs the next. When I began working part-time, I cleaned Friday afternoons and finished up on Saturday morning with the help of the children. When I work full-time, the kids and I clean on Saturday morning or afternoon, whichever works out best that particular day.

Even though I have a half-day on Saturday set aside for my weekly cleaning, the actual number of hours available varies drastically from week to week. I may have from 8-12 which is plenty of time to do my regular list of chores, plus extra for folding laundry and a break to read the morning mail and make a few phone calls.

Sometimes the morning is slightly shortened by running errands, phone calls, and church and family activities. I have to keep moving right along and do things less thoroughly — dusting only the tops of furniture, sweeping but not washing the kitchen floor. And sometimes my morning is practically wiped out by heavy commitments like a wedding or a women's quiet day at church. This calls for a really quick job — dusting, vacuuming and a quick touch-up of the bathrooms and kitchen. On a weekend like this, I may ask the kids to do a little extra to help me.

Occasionally I am free the whole day and can take my cleaning at a more leisurely pace, attacking some extra jobs that need doing, such as cleaning the oven or straightening the mittens in the front closet, deciding what old magazines to throw out, moving my winter clothes and getting out summer things or washing out the wastebaskets and trash barrels. It is a luxury to have a day like that!

When the time comes to clean, I like to hit the whole house at once, with everyone helping. Ideally after breakfast on Saturday, the kids and I get the cleaning supplies out and all work at once — each one doing his or her assigned jobs. When our schedules are not all free at the same time, I usually set a deadline for when they are to have their area completed: "Before you leave for the party" or "By lunch time." This way, each one is clear about what is expected. Of course, when my children were younger, I did all the cleaning myself — and now, before I know it, they will be gone, and I will be doing it alone again. Adjustments are required, as we move through the various stages of our lives.

It is time to clean! But remember: this is your weekly upkeep — not a thorough "spring cleaning." Don't go overboard on any one area. If you spend two hours on one bathroom, nothing else will get done.

Let's go through the basic steps:

1. Get out cleaning supplies

Set out in a centrally located place:
— cleaning rags
— spray window cleaner*
— heavy duty spray spot cleaner*
— furniture wax or polish or spray
— dust mop or broom
— vacuum cleaner and tools

*Use pump rather than aerosol sprays when possible, so as not to worsen the ozone problem that the environmentalists are so concerned about. Also, spray nozzles break and clog too easily, causing waste.

2. Do a general pick up

Before you clean, go around each room and pick up and *put away* clutter — toys, magazines, snack plates, school books — whatever is out of place. Beds should be made up and clothes placed in closets and drawers or tossed in the laundry basket. It is easiest to do the whole house or one floor at a time. Carry a bag with you for collecting trash and emptying wastebaskets.

3. Change the beds, if they are done at this time of week

Actually, I prefer to change the beds the day before I clean, so that I don't have to do everything at once. But that may not be convenient for you. I strip the beds in the morning and remake them at bedtime. I can either lay out a second set of sheets before I leave for work, or, by putting in a load of laundry before and after work, I can remake the beds with the same sheets. Years ago, I could never have allowed myself this freedom, but now I consider not making the beds one morning a week a little treat. Also, re-making beds goes *much* quicker if more than one person is involved, and this way I usually have my husband and/or my children to help. If you prefer to do the beds on the same day as you clean, the beds should be done right after your general pick-up.

4. Spot clean with spray glass cleaner

Excluding the bathrooms, which will be done separately, go from room to room with a nice dry towel and spray glass cleaner. Spray and buff dry:
— mirrors
— painted wood surfaces (mantle, painted shelves or dresser, window sills,
      as necessary)
— plastic (record player lid) and vinyl
— glass (hurricane lamp shades, picture glass)
— formica counters
— kitchen cupboard doors, as needed
— appliances
— using your damp cloth, wipe picture frame edges.

5. Spot clean with a heavier cleaner

Heavy duty spray cleaners need to be wiped immediately and not allowed to make drip marks. Again, go from room to room, doing all the house in one sweep. Basically look for fingerprints, scrapes, and smears on door casings, and walls and corners in heavy traffic areas.

6. Water plants

Go around the house, watering all the plants adequately. If you are a gifted gardener, you will have a better feel for how often different plants will need to be watered in your home. It varies according to the time of year and the heat and humidity in the house. I water them all once a week, whether they need it or not! (Obviously God did not give me a green thumb.)

7. Care for wood furniture

Using spray polish or wax or lemon oil, go through the house, polishing and dusting your natural-finish wood furniture. Be sure you are utilizing the best product for your pieces. I used a propellant polish which over a period of years caused smearing problems on the finish. I called a store which sold that particular brand, and they were able to straighten me out on what I should use and how I could best repair the damage. Now I use lemon oil on my best furniture and spray polish on my inexpensive pieces which need more wax. Do the tops, and if more time is available, do sides, edges, fronts, shelves and legs. This may involve removing things from the top surface and then replacing them. As you go along, wipe knick-knacks with a cloth damp with glass cleaner.

8. Do rugs and floors

The rooms are basically done, and the final step is the rugs and floors. Use a dust mop or broom on floors, sweeping crumbs and debris onto the nearest rug. Then vacuum all the rugs. (As I've indicated, I do not move large pieces of furniture each week.) See where the rug needs vacuuming, and be as thorough as possible without going overboard. If necessary, finish up by washing the floors. How you do this depends on the manufacturer's directions. Many floors today required only sponging with soap and water or just water. I prefer doing it on my hands and knees and drying with a towel as I go. Some weeks there won't be time to wash the whole floor, so check for spots and spills.

9. Do the bathrooms

Bathrooms call for some different supplies, so I usually do them all at once and separately from the cleaning of the other rooms. It works well to keep the cleaning supplies together in a commode under one of the sinks, in a plastic tub or tray.
   — use glass cleaner on mirrors
   — use spot cleaner on fingerprints and spots — doors, drawer fronts
   — spray sinks, vanities, and toilets (inside and out) with a foam bathroom cleaner. Wipe with sponge or with a towel. The inner part of the toilet bowl can be wiped with a sponge or with a long-handled brush.
   — clean the tub or shower with spray foam bathroom cleaner. Occasionally use a stronger foam to remove calcium deposits and water marks.
   — wash the floor or vacuum the rug

Before washing the floor, I usually run the vacuum over it or use the dust mop to sweep the hair and debris out onto the hall rug, where it can be easily vacuumed up. A heavy-duty spray cleaner works well on a tile floor, leaving no sticky residue to pick up new smears. Vinyl floors must be cleaned according to manufacturer's directions — soap and water, a cleaner, or a special floor preparation.

10. Put cleaning supplies away

You are done! Put away the vacuum, store the cleaners and polishes in a handy closet, toss the dirty rags in the laundry basket.

For a rule of thumb, if you find you cannot follow these steps and clean your house in two to four uninterrupted hours, you are doing more than is necessary for regular weekly cleaning. Compare what you do with the lists, and see where you are spending too much time. Work towards getting your time down to a more manageable level. It will be easier to begin, if you know that your goal is possible.

All of this is definitely work. It sometimes takes real strength of will to get started, or to persevere until it is done. Don't expect to be able to make yourself do it all on your own. Ask Jesus to help you, where you feel weak or resistant, or primed to be distracted by any "legitimate" excuse. One of the fastest answers to prayer comes in response to the one that begins: "Lord, please change my heart." Try it! Tell Him how much you loathe swabbing out the bottoms of the garbage cans (or whatever the job happens to be). He already knows how you feel, but you still have to tell Him, and acknowledge that you know He wants you to do them. Then, ask Him to change your heart about the job, and watch what happens! You may not ever love doing it, but you won't mind it.

Another thing I do is put on a Christian record that lifts my spirits and gets me going. Try that, too; you might find yourself singing you way through the house. A bit noisy, perhaps, but effective.

At this point in my life, my children work along with me. On most Saturday mornings, you will find my son Kirk cleaning his room and listening to a sports show. My grade school daughter Joy would be cleaning the hamster cage and singing along to a Kid's Praise tape. Michelle, a teenager who shares our home, could be found in the bathroom, scrubbing and polishing in time to the Amy Grant music from her earphones. Where would I be? Down in the kitchen shining up the appliances and singing something like "Climb Every Mountain." And hopefully, by lunchtime, we will be finished and free to do other things.

9

What To Do When You Have Only a Few Minutes

"I'm going on a retreat for two days, and right after I get home, my Bible Study group is coming over."

"I have a million errands to do! I won't be home for longer than an hour at a time, and Sunday evening John's folks are coming for dinner."

These situations happen to all of us. We have "no" time but want the house to look decent. It is amazing how much can be accomplished in a 30-to-60 minute speed-cleaning, working alone or with everybody pitching in.

Pick Up & Straighten. This is the most important step! Put things away. Throw things away. Close closet doors. Shut cupboard and doors.

Dust. Use a rag slightly damp with the polish, wax or oil you use and quickly go through the house dusting top surfaces of furniture. With another rag damp with glass cleaner, wipe other surfaces. This is not a careful, thorough polishing — just a quick spruce-up. Don't do much bending or stretching; stick to eye level stuff.

Sweep. Sweep debris off floors onto rugs. Wipe up any noticeable spots or spills with a damp sponge and dry with a towel.

Vacuum. Vacuum all rugs quickly, hitting the main traffic patterns and where you actually see lint and crumbs.

Bathrooms. Give a quick spray of window cleaner to mirrors and wipe off with a towel. Spray bathroom cleaner in toilets, in sinks, and on vanities. Wipe surfaces with sponge or coarse-sided scrub sponge. Flush toilets. Wipe surfaces dry with a towel. And you're done!

Of course, such a speed-cleaning is made all the easier by good, regular daily upkeep of the house. If you don't let it get too far ahead of you, you won't have as much of a mess to work your way through. So, make the beds, empty wastebaskets, do the dishes, and pick up once a day.

69

There are really two areas of concern involved here: how do you feel about the house yourself, and how do you think other people judge your housekeeping. It is easy to get tangled up in self-condemnation and guilt, in feelings of competition and inferiority.

"In the old days" I had to have the house picture-perfect when someone came over. Now God has taught me how to let go of my demands. I still enjoy a neat and clean home, ready for company, with just the right lamps turned on to show every room at its best and all the rugs freshly vacuumed. Often, though, people will drop by unexpectedly, when I am in the middle of a sewing project down in the basement, or when I haven't done the dinner dishes yet and am practicing the piano. They don't seem to mind. The place is not a disaster — it is just where my family lives.

We each need the Lord to teach us how to do enough and not too much — to clean the house so that host and guest both feel comfortable. To do *too little* can leave the host feeling guilty and the guest embarrassed. To do *too much* will leave the host over-tired and on edge, and the guest intimidated by the neatness and deciding never to invite such a perfectionist over to his or her home.

You need to be open to what the Lord tells you about when and how much to clean. And then be able to relax and be at peace with what you have done. Recognize your motives, and confess them when they are wrong. And ask Jesus to help you to care more for the people who enter your home, than for what they think about you.

PRAYER:
Dear Lord,

I need your help. I'm trying to clean the house, and I just can't seem to get it the way I want it. I confess I haven't asked You for guidance. Please forgive me and show me what to do in the time I have left. I confess my motives aren't pure. I've been trying to (impress someone, show I am a good housekeeper, prove I can clean as well as so-and-so, etc.) I ask for Your forgiveness and Your bloodwashing. Help me to relax in what You show me to do and to care for my guest as I would care for You, if You visited our home. Thank You, Lord. Amen.

10

What About the Children?

"Parents, do not treat your children in such a way as to make them angry. Instead, raise them with Christian discipline and instruction."

— *Ephesians 6:4*

Should children help around the house? Absolutely! I couldn't do it without them. Even if I had more free time, or if I had money enough to hire someone, I still would have them help.

Contributing their time and effort to help keep their home in good shape is important. Children need to learn to take responsibility, to share their part in the load. In addition, they will acquire valuable skills for life-long use.

It may seem easier to just do it yourself, but it isn't! At first, it does require more time, as you teach a new skill, and as you follow-up, to make sure the job is completed correctly. Eventually, though, they will be able to make a significant contribution. It takes effort to encourage them and be supportive of their efforts. And it is difficult to find that proper balance of making sure the kids do a good job, without setting unreasonably high standards. But believe me — it is worth the effort — for you and for them.

When I was growing up, I complained about any jobs I was asked to do, crying the blues about all the homework I had to do, or about my heavy load of babysitting and school activities. In fact, I managed to make myself such a pain in the neck, it is no wonder my mother was glad when I went to my room. I had to help with the dishes, and I also remember vacuuming the hallway steps and making my bed; however, I did not really take any regular responsibility for the house. I just did whatever little jobs I was given. After all, cleaning the house was my mother's job; I had school. What a narrow, selfish view I had! I didn't see the wider picture of all the things my mother did outside the home — church work, charitable work, involvements with my school and caring for friends and relatives. I just saw what was inconvenient for me. Occasionally I would help do a big job like clean the garage or rake leaves, but generally, I avoided housework as much as possible.

God brings all kinds of circumstances into our lives, to change us and mold us. I might have allowed my kids to be as I had been, but God seemed to be calling to be involved in more than I could handle. I needed help. John and I sought guidance in prayer and from close Christian friends, gradually seeing God's plan for us as a family. Kirk and Joy do have their school work as a first priority, but they have learned how to balance responsibilities in all the areas of their lives. Doing jobs around the house, practicing their instruments, caring for their pets, and playing with their friends all have a place.

Where do you begin? I give each child regular daily and weekly chores. As they grow, their assignments change to reflect their abilities. Joy, who is nine, empties the upstairs wastebaskets every morning before school, as well as makes her bed and picks up her room. On Saturdays, she helps change her bed, cleans the hamster cage, and does the wastebaskets in the whole house. (Even as I write this, I can see she needs to be helping a little more. I have the common problem of seeing my youngest as younger than she is.)

Before school, Kirk (14) feeds his cat, makes his bed, picks up his room and washes the breakfast dishes. In the evening, he takes his turn doing dishes and sometimes helps Joy with her homework. His weekly responsibilities are to clean the cat box, vacuum the rugs in the basement and clean his room and the family room (pick up, dust and vacuum). Of course, there are many jobs they do on call (unloading groceries is a big one!) There are seasonal jobs, too — we have a yard full of trees and lots of fall raking, as well as plenty of snow to shovel in the winter. When I do my big cleaning, I teach them how to go through the storage areas in their own rooms — throwing out, giving away and straightening (a valuable lesson!).

Here is a list of jobs children can do. I have arranged it roughly in ascending order of difficulty. Add your own ideas to it.

- picking up toys
- emptying wastebaskets
- carrying laundry to laundry area
- picking up own room
- making beds
- putting away dry dishes or emptying dishwasher
- delivering clean laundry to the proper rooms
- putting away their own laundry
- setting the table for dinner
- helping clear the table after a meal
- cleaning a pet's cage
- cleaning the inside of car windows and the dash board
- drying dishes
- bagging piles of raked up leaves in the yard
- cleaning out their own drawers and shelves twice a year
- fixing the beverages for dinner
- washing dishes

— making tossed salad
— cleaning their own room weekly
— vacuuming, in the house or inside the car
— making lunches to carry to school
— raking the lawn
— mowing the lawn
— folding laundry
— washing the car
— simple ironing
— helping cook meals

Others:

—
—
—
—
—
—

The next step is to pray about your own children and what they should be doing. Once you have settled on their chores, be sure to regularly re-evaluate them.

Child's Name	Daily Jobs	Weekly Jobs	Special Projects

Child's Name	Daily Job	Weekly Job	Special Projects

11

The Laundry Is Piled Up Again!

How do you handle the laundry? Some people do it every day, throwing in a load or two before they leave for work, or while their youngsters are watching "Sesame Street". Maybe you are a person who has a specific day when you wash everything, as well as doing folding and ironing. Others do laundry on an "as needed" basis — putting it off as long as possible and then doing it the night before everyone runs out of clean underwear.

The needs of a family ebb and flow, greater at one time, less at another. Babies generate lots of dirty clothes; so do football players of all ages. A family of four children will definitely keep the washer and dryer busier than a family with one child, unless the one is a teenager who is going through a stage where a clothing change seems to be necessary every 30 minutes!

The important thing when considering your laundry, is to make a conscious decision. As elsewhere, step back and evaluate the situation. Use prayer, careful thinking and creative planing. The problem is that usually we just fall into doing things a certain way, catch as catch can. Often it is not the most efficient way. Trust God to guide you to the best choice for you and your family.

In the early years of our marriage, I did laundry once a week. Later, when the kids were little, I fell into the "do a little every day" pattern. Once there were no more babies, I did not need to do it that often, but I never made a change in a new schedule.

At that point I took a look at how I was handling the laundry, and how I felt about it. I realized that I was basically attempting to keep it always done and up-to-date. How ridiculous! I had set an impossible goal for myself. Instead of feeling good because I was keeping the laundry basket empty, I was feeling bad because the ping-pong table (my laundry, sewing, and craft projects area) always had some clothes on it. I was never *done!*

At that point, I decided to do laundry three days a week: Monday, Thursday, and Friday. Only on those days would I take dirty things down. My commitment was to keep things moving along on each of those days, and once they were completed, not to start more until the next laundry day.

Folding and delivering clean clothes are little jobs I squeeze in between major things on my schedule. After breakfast and before I leave for work are prime times for putting loads in, or even for doing some quick folding. While dinner is cooking, or while the kids do the dishes, I have a few more minutes to work on it — and maybe while I catch part of the news on TV.

Ironing takes a little longer and needs to be allowed for on your schedule. I enjoy watching a one-hour TV show while I iron — a nice, peaceful time from 9 to 10 P.M., usually when I don't really have the initiative to do anything else.

Establish a place where you can neatly hang or lay things waiting to be ironed; that way, the clutter won't always be annoying you and making you feel guilty.

Thursdays I would do all the towels and washcloths, putting out clean ones on all the racks and hooks that day; and *Fridays* I would strip the beds and do all the sheets.

In general I have kept this system, although I am not legalistic about which exact days I wash. I do stick to the "towel day" and the "sheet day". Of course, there are still those weeks when all the clean clothes get piled up in a mountain on the table, and I have to send the kids down on a treasure hunt for underwear, when it is time to get dressed. That's just one of the hazards of family life!

Decide what you will do to make your laundry less of a burden. Choose your days. Get your children involved — first, with delivering clean clothes, later with folding, and finally with ironing. These are valuable skills. Select a day to do your towels and your bed linens, and work it into your overall cleaning schedule.

My laundry plan will be to: (explain briefly — every day, specific days, once a week, etc.)

I will do towels on: (day)   **I will do sheets on:** (day)

12

Checking Wardrobes

Shoppers come in all shapes and sizes. One friend of mine looks for that perfect dress for a special event. She may spend several evenings or Saturdays searching through numerous stores, before making her final selection. Another friend, with a very busy schedule and very little time, takes a different approach. When she needs new clothes, she prays that God will bless and direct her shopping and takes off on a flying tour through her favorite stores. Almost literally grabbing outfits as she goes, she comes home with some surprisingly great buys. Someone else might hate to shop so much that they put it off as long as possible — until they literally have nothing decent to wear. (Husbands are more notorious for this attitude than wives.) Most of us fall somewhere in between these extremes.

Having had a weight problem most of my adult life, buying clothes was really a low priority. There weren't many choices in my size, and the whole endeavor was depressing, so I put it off as long as I could. Then, when I did shop, I used to buy the first thing that fit. But buying for our home was a different matter. God had given me a gift for interior decorating, and I always enjoyed purchasing items to make the house look good. This is the way I was for years — splurging on the house and on gifts, scrimping on myself. (I discovered that I felt I didn't really deserve nice clothes!)

When the Lord came into my life, this pattern was one He gradually began to change. People close to me, whose input I asked for and trusted, helped me to see that punishing myself with hastily-purchased, dull, unstylish clothes was not God's way. I also realized I didn't really know what looked most flattering on me. The first time my friend Laurie helped me pick out a new outfit — dress, shoes, jewelry — I felt beautiful! For years afterward, whenever I put that dress on, tears of joy and gratefulness would sting my eyes. So having help was the first step. I also learned to look for stores and departments that carried more things in my size — and the tall lengths I needed. It's amazing how good I feel, when I wear something that fits comfortably and is attractive. It frees me to be more outgoing and less self-conscious.

Wardrobe care involves planning, especially if you sew. You need to prepare for the seasons, before they arrive. Summer and winter are good times to look ahead, to watch newspaper ads for the sales and to purchase patterns and material for projects you want to complete for spring-summer or for fall-winter wear. Go through your present wardrobe and check fit and condition. Make necessary repairs. Write down things you need to complete your wardrobe. Consider special events you will be attending, and what you will wear. If you need to purchase items to match things you currently own, carry the items in a handy bag, so you can check for coordination as you shop. Set times in your schedule (use special project times) to go shopping. And if you need help, take a friend who is gifted in selecting attractive clothes. Use your list and have an idea of the amount of money you are able to spend. **Make a plan — use it!**

This space is for you to use in planning for next season.

Clothes Needing Repairs

Items to Purchase for Repairs

Items Needed to Match Current Outfits
(clothes, accessories, shoes, jewelry)

Item To Take To Check Coordination

Additions Planned for My Wardrobe

Sew or Purchase?

The crunch comes when you also have children to think about. They are always growing and changing! Oh, how we can complain about needing to buy them new clothes every year! A good safety valve is to remember that their growth is God's gift. (Think how unhappy you would be, if they stopped!)

Shopping with children can be a real nightmare. You are busy trying to compare prices and quality, while your teenager wanders off to the shoe department and your four-year-old hides under the rack of coats and only giggles when you call her name. The kids may love new clothes, but they hate to try things on. The little ones tire of it after two outfits and assure you that everything fits no matter what sizes they are, while the teenager insists that nothing fits and they look horrible in everything. Your son wants to carry his own bag of new clothes, and then somehow, mysteriously manages to lose it somewhere in the mall between Sears and Penney's! You may not be able to avoid such incidents, but it does help to plan ahead.

Whether you are at home full-time or work outside the home, keeping up-to-date with the clothes for the children is a job that requires organization. I have found it works well to shop twice a year: *before Easter,* for spring-summer wear, and *before school starts,* for fall-winter clothing. I want to avoid a store full of rushed parents and harried salespeople, and I want a good selection to choose from, so I shop towards the beginning to middle of Lent and again in late July. It is nice to purchase that new Easter dress when the stock is not picked over, and since we go on summer vacation in August, it is good to come home, knowing we are pretty well set for the opening of school.

How do you begin to plan your child's wardrobe?

1. Use a tape measure and take measurements. Compare these to size charts, as in mail order catalogs, to figure out the child's sizes — dress, shirts, slacks, shoes, etc.

2. Check his or her present wardrobe. See what still fits. Pack up outgrown clothes to store for younger children in the family, or to pass on to friends or charitable organizations. If you're keeping them, decide on a convenient place to put hand-me-downs. Occasionally you need to check what you have saved; maybe your daughter has had a growth spurt and needs some longer skirts. Or perhaps there is some unusually warm spring weather, and suddenly everyone wants to wear shorts. If you have saved them but can't find things, they will be wasted.

3. Assess what is left and what is needed to make the wardrobe sufficient for the child's needs. Make lists of *needs* and *wants*. From these, plan a reasonable shopping list.

4. If you do sewing for your children, this is the time to get started. Purchase materials, patterns and notions and begin work. Have a general idea of when you plan to sew (check your schedule), and when things need to be completed. But be careful you don't overestimate the amount you can handle. It is better to complete two outfits you feel good about, than to do four poorly, or to be left with two items unfinished and insufficient yardage to make a bigger size next year.

5. (This step is a personal preference and a great time-saver.) Use mail order catalogs. Go through them yourself and with the older children, looking at what is available in their size. Use sale catalogs as much as possible. (If you order regularly, you will receive these in the mail.) Mark items to be ordered. When you have done this for each child, you will be ready to call in your order. I like to have it delivered to my home by UPS, as the stores are not in my neighborhood.

When the children were young, I was able to purchase most of their clothes in this way. For boys especially, I found much more variety in the catalogs. As they have gotten older and have more personal choices about their outfits, as well as being a little harder to fit, I have ordered fewer things, but continue to find the catalogs have the widest selection in underclothes, socks, pajamas and school slacks.

After the delivery arrives, have each child try on the items. Check for size, quality, and style. If necessary, reorder the article of clothing in another size to get a better fit, making plans to return the original item when you are next out shopping. (Don't make a special trip!)

6. Make plans to shop in stores for the rest of the clothes. Even when catalogs are used extensively, it is still good to shop in person for clothes for a special occasion, for hard-to-fit items (slacks, shoes, etc.), and for a chance to see what styles most flatter your child's shape and coloring. Shopping can be enjoyable, if you have only a small number of items to purchase.

Set a time on your schedule to take each child shopping separately. Make it a special time for you and your son or daughter — a time to shop, to talk, to go out for lunch or a snack together. It is only twice a year, so make an occasion of it! Be sure to take along any items that require matching.

As I have mentioned before, I am not a dedicated shopper. I used to just make my list and head through the mall, quickly making purchases. These shopping trips, however, have become special times for me with my children. Joy doesn't really like to try on the clothes, but she loves going out to lunch with "just Mommy." As Kirk has gotten older, Dad has been taking over the shopping, and it is good to see them having this project to do together.

7. Always keep birthdays and Christmas in mind, as you shop. Will you be giving some gifts of clothes, or will they be receiving any from grandparents? If so, *don't over-buy*. Maybe you will notice your child particularly likes a certain outfit or style. Purchase it and put it away for later, as a gift.

My son's birthday is in October. Although he gets his school clothes in July, his birthday is a nice time for a ski sweater or a special long-sleeved shirt. For Christmas, I like to make or buy a special outfit for my daughter. (Grandparents are notoriously wonderful about giving such fancy ensembles! Make sure you don't duplicate expense and effort.)

8. Watch end-of-season sales for good buys. Though I am not particularly good at following sales, I have been able to get some winter coats at half price to put aside for next year. This has allowed me to purchase top-quality items that would normally be out of our price range.

I remember one March when the zipper on Joy's winter jacket broke. I was furious! A whole month of winter left and no coat! We checked the local ski shop, which carries gorgeous, top-quality coats that I would normally never buy. It was the end-of-season 40%-50% off sale, and we got a lavender jacket Joy loved. We purchased a larger size, and she was able to wear it two more winters.

The point of all this is: **plan ahead.** Don't wait until the week before school begins or the day before Easter. Don't shop with all of your children at once — the four-year-old pulling tags off all the dresses on the rack, the nine-year-old whining about having to try on dresses, and the teenager complaining about even having to be seen with such babies! What a disaster! Mark a date on your calendar to start making plans for the children. Then when that times comes, follow through. Do one child at a time.

Clothes Needing Repairs	**Items to Purchase for Repairs or Alterations**

81

**Items to Take
to Match Current Outfits**

**Items Needed
to Check Coordination**

Additions to Wardrobe   **Catalog or Store?**   **Sew or Purchase?**

13

Entertaining

Entertaining — is that a word that brings fear to your heart? Do you love having people over? Or do you avoid it at all cost? Or are you in between, always thinking you would like to entertain more, but somehow never get around to it?

Let's face it: entertaining is work. It doesn't just effortlessly happen. As you read this chapter, ask God to help you see what He would have you do in this area.

What kind of entertaining do you presently do?

What are your spouse's or roommate's preferences in this area?

What things would you like to do that you haven't done?

What stops you from entertaining?

When it comes to entertaining, God has definitely given us different gifts and different styles. Some like formal dinner parties, while others prefer a family picnic. One couple loves to have pool parties, while another likes to have a casual buffet supper, followed by a home video movie. A person may have a special talent for organizing wedding or baby showers. Someone else may enjoy arranging a night out at a concert, followed by a yummy dessert at home.

I mentioned at the outset that before I became a Christian, I thought the only way to entertain was to serve multi-course dinners. I still enjoy doing that occasionally, but now find myself also involved in a variety of types of entertaining, such as several families together for an evening meal during the week, the junior high fellowship pizza party, or a surprise shower for a friend with a new home. And I go in spurts. But there is a freedom to flow from one to another, as I feel God directing me.

Entertaining changes with one's age and situation. Are you into grammar school birthday parties? Or a formal dinner for your "sweet sixteen" daughter? How about planning a wedding, with all that entails, or maybe having your friends over for lunch, now that your schedule is more free? There is a time and a season for everything.

Whom do you invite? I find God bringing ideas to my mind which answer a whole gamut of needs. A friend and I, for instance, need to get together for lunch occasionally, or our friendship won't be kept current. Our commitments have changed, and without these specific appointments, we rarely have time to share deeply about what is going on in our lives. Old friends we have not seen for a while often come to mind. It is good to catch up. Introducing old friends to new friends is fun — and a wonderful way to build a sense of family in a neighborhood or in a church. There are so many possibilities — people you work with, people you see a lot but have never really gotten to know, families whose children are the same ages as yours, mixtures of people you know, who don't know each other. And, of course, there is your extended family — grandparents, uncles, aunts, cousins. It is especially important to be open to God's leading, when considering your family.

Before you start worrying about the effort involved, catch the vision of what you are to do. Should you have a fancy dinner party once in a while, using all your prettiest tableware? Are you supposed to commit yourself to do some kind of entertaining once a month? Maybe a small luncheon for a few friends would be more your style.

Once you have sensed the direction in which you should go, don't approach it as a fate worse than death! Just take it step by step.

1. Check your schedule for a good date. Choose a date when you will have time to prepare and clean up without being too pushed. Don't box yourself in with a party in the midst of an already busy week.

2. Invite the guests. Call or write them far enough ahead to give plenty of notice. Don't take it personally and get hurt, if they are unable to attend. Most people enjoy being included and are genuinely disappointed when there is a conflict.

3. Plan the menu a week ahead, as well as a plan of attack. Sit down and take adequate time to plan the menu and make your grocery list. Look at your calendar and jot down your plan for getting things done. It might look like this:

Thursday, March 28: grocery shop
Friday, March 29: 7-10 p.m., make frozen dessert, soup, appetizers, and stuff potatoes
Saturday, March 30: morning - make dough for rolls
                   set table
         afternoon - do regular weekly house cleaning
         5:00 p.m. - meat in oven
          6-7 p.m. - final preparations
         7:00 p.m. - Dinner Party

4. Don't overdo it! Depending on how well you cook, use only one or two new or fussy recipes. Rely on dependable old favorites, until you feel more comfortable with the entertaining. There are two important truths to keep in mind about the food you serve, no matter what it is:
a.) The women will enjoy it because someone else did the work.
b.) Even a disaster isn't so bad. One rarely destroys the whole meal, so a burned-up appetizer is nothing to get upset about. The meat was a little tough, but everything else was great. If you relax with it, so will your guests.

5. Spend as much time as possible with your guests. Try to avoid a menu that keeps you in the kitchen all evening. Keep the purpose of the meal in mind. It is to get to know each other better, not to show off your culinary skills. Being together is more important than the food.

Listen to what God is saying to you about entertaining. What goal should you set for yourself?

Now, list the names of people God is nudging you to include:

On the next few pages you will find menus and recipes I have often used. The directions are not too involved and the results usually taste great!

A Weeknight Meal to Share with Another Family

Mom's Meat Loaf*
Fresh Green Beans
Baked Potatoes
Applesauce
Milk-Tea-Coffee-Ice Water
Mint Chocolate Lime Dessert*
recipes follow

Make it simple, satisfying and tasty, and everybody is sure to enjoy the meal. Set your table attractively — just using colorful cloth or paper napkins will make it look festive. A plant or a bouquet of flowers is a nice centerpiece.

On a weeknight, adults and children often have meetings to attend — church committees, choir, Boy & Girl Scouts, classes, PTA, and so on. Because of this, dinner is rarely an all-evening proposition — one to one and a half hours is usual. Enjoy the time you have, and then go on with the rest of your evening.

We eat every Wednesday with two other families, rotating houses. It's great! I only have to cook every third week, and the fellowship around the table is lively and fun.

Recipe

Mom's Meat Loaf

2 pounds ground chuck
1 egg
4 handfuls of crumbled Wheaties
1 medium onion chopped + 3 slices for garnishing
½ c. ketchup and a few T. milk

Mix thoroughly with hands. Smooth and shape into an oval loaf. Place in a 9″ x 13″ pan. Go over the surface with a wet knife to smooth all rough spots. (This eliminates little openings where fat can collect during cooking, causing the loaf to crumble when sliced.)
Bake at 375 degrees for one hour.

Mint Chocolate Lime Dessert

2 round layers of plain chocolate cake
1 pint lime sherbet
½ c. chocolate chips

1 T. margarine
1½ t. milk
1½ t. light corn syrup

Slice each cake layer in half horizontally to form two thinner layers. Starting with a layer of cake, alternate cake and sherbet, ending with the fourth layer of cake. Freeze.

Make mint glaze by melting together chocolate chips, margarine, milk, and corn syrup. Stir constantly until smooth. Spread on top of cake. Return to freezer.

Let stand out of freezer ten minutes before serving.

Saturday Night Dinner Party

Cranberry Shrub*
Cheese Triangles*
Bacon-Mushroom Appetizers*
Cherry Soup*
Romaine Salad*
Chicken Cordon Bleu*
Long Grain & Wild Rice
Fresh Asparagus or Broccoli
Rolls
Tea-Coffee-Ice Water
Trifle*

Use all your best china and glasses, cloth napkins and candles. I've noticed that even meat loaf tastes fancy, served on china by candlelight!

Serve the appetizers and punch in the living room or family room. The first course at the table is the soup, followed by the salad, the main course, and, finally, the dessert. If you want to leave out a course, delete the soup.

Take your time. Enjoy each course. Some people like to finish the meal, and then play a game, such as Trivial Pursuit. John and I aren't game fans; we treasure the time to sit over after-dinner coffee and have uninterrupted time to talk.

You may wonder what we do with Kirk and Joy during an evening for adults only. I usually invite the company to arrive at 7:30 p.m. The kids eat TV dinners (they love them!) earlier and enjoy watching television upstairs in a bedroom, or down in the basement. When they were little, I had them all ready for bed right after their dinner so I just had to go up quickly, when it was time for them to turn out the lights.

Recipes

Cheese Triangles

6 oz. crabmeat, thawed
1 stick butter or margarine
½ lb. Velvetta cheese
English muffins

Melt and stir the first three ingredients together. Split the muffins and spread with the hot mixture. Broil. Cut each half roll into 6 small wedges and serve.

You can broil these ahead. When they are cool, wrap in foil. Reheat at 350 degrees for 10 minutes right before serving.

Bacon-Mushroom Squares

1 lb. cooked bacon, crumbled
½ lb. mushrooms (canned stems and pieces)
6 oz. American cheese, grated or diced
6 oz. Swiss cheese, grated or diced
⅔ c. mayonnaise

Mix all the ingredients and mound on party rye. Bake at 350 degrees until bubbly.

Cranberry Shrub

Cranberry Juice Cocktail
Raspberry sherbert

Fill the punch cup or glass ⅔'s with juice. Add a small scoop of sherbet.

Romaine Salad

2 heads of romaine
¼ lb. bacon, cooked and crumbled
1 c. grated swiss cheese (3 oz.)
⅔ c. toasted almonds
⅓ c. parmesan cheese
1 c. croutons (fried in left over bacon drippings)

Mix the salad. Just before serving toss with this dressing:

juice of one lemon
¾ c. salad oil
3 cloves garlic

(Let this mixture set for three hours before putting on salad.)

Cherry Soup

1 lb. water-pack red sour pitted cherries
¼ c. sugar
2 T. cornstarch
¼ t. salt
¼ t. cinnamon
½ c. orange juice

Blend the above ingredients in a blender. Pour into saucepan and cook over medium heat, stirring until it boils. Boil, stirring for ½ minute. Remove from heat. Stir in ½ c. red wine (cooking or regular).

Serve hot or chilled. Garnish with a dollop of whipped cream.

Chicken Cordon Bleu

3 chicken breasts, boned and skinned (makes 6 pieces)
3 slices of swiss cheese
3 slices of boiled ham
2 T. margarine
1 c. chicken broth
½ c. milk or ½ c. white wine
chopped parsley

Pound chicken to flatten. Place ½ slice cheese and ½ slice ham on each breast. Roll up and secure with a toothpick. Pour liquid and margarine over all. Sprinkle with parsley. Bake at 350 degrees for one hour.

Trifle

Layer the following items in glass bowl, in this order:
— broken up yellow cake or lady fingers spread with raspberry jam
— vanilla pudding
— drained, sliced canned pears
— another later of jam and bread
— vanilla pudding
— pears
— layer of whipped cream
— sprinkle with almond slices

A Saturday Wedding Brunch or Baby Shower

Cranberry Punch*
Croissant Sandwiches*
Spinach Salad*
Tea-Coffee
Fresh Fruit Cup

Invite your guests to arrive at 10 or 11 a.m. While people are coming, serve the punch. A few simple games might be the next order of business. Look at card and gift shops for books of ideas with wedding or baby themes, and have cute gifts for prizes — a mug, an unusual potholder, a bookmark, a potted plant.

Now it is time for the guest of honor to open her gifts. Be sure someone sits nearby and keeps an accurate list of presenters and their presents. At a wedding shower, a bridesmaid should have a paper plate with a hole in the middle to make a ribbon bouquet for the rehearsal.

The party ends with the meal. Have a buffet table set up with a platter of croissant sandwiches, a bowl of spinach salad, as well as silverware, napkins, tea and coffee. Guests can hold their plates in their laps. If your table is large enough, you can have a sit-down meal. As they are finishing, offer more croissants and salad. After you have removed the plates, serve cups of cut-up fresh fruit.

Recipe

Cranberry Punch

Combine and chill: 4 c. cranberry juice
4 c. pineapple juice
1 T. almond extract

Add 2 liters of ginger ale or 7-Up.
Serve.

Croissant Sandwiches

4 bakery croissants
2 T. mayonnaise
½ lb. thinly sliced roast beef
4 slices meunster cheese
8 medium or 12 small slices tomato

Slice croissants in half horizontally to form a top and a bottom. (Slice gently with serrated knife.) Spread a little mayonnaise on each bottom half. Arrange roast beef on roll — fold beef to fit the croissant. Top beef with cheese, and be careful not to let the cheese extend over sides of the roll. Lay on two or three slices of tomato. Put on the top half of the roll. Place the four sandwiches in a 9″ x 13″ pan. Cover lightly with foil. Heat at 250 degrees for 15 minutes. Slice into two halves and serve.

Spinach Salad

1 lb. torn up fresh spinach
½ hard boiled egg per person
thinly sliced onion
crumbled, cooked bacon, if desired

Dressing: ½ c. mayonnaise
3 T. vinegar
¼ c. sugar
⅓ c. half and half

A Tea Party for Little Girls

Tea
Milk & Sugar
Cut-up Fruit on Toothpicks
Sandwiches in Fancy Shapes
Cheese Cubes
Tiny Cookies

Whenever Joy has someone over for the afternoon, I'm sure to hear, "Can we have a tea party, please, Mom?" Use a child-sized tea set to make this especially fun for your daughter and her friends.

One year on her birthday, we just expanded the idea. The girls were asked to dress in their Sunday best. As I drove from house to house, Kirk, spiffed up in his suit, called at the door and gave each young lady a flower and then escorted her to the car. (It took a little convincing to get him to help, but it did end up being fun!) I had the dining room table all set with my best china, and after taking pictures of each one, the girls enjoyed their tea.

Once I had served, I made myself scarce, but I noticed they were very polite to each other and had a good time "talking." For genteel activity, we went outside for a game of croquet. Later, I gave each set of parents a copy of the picture I had taken of their daughter.

Recipe

Sandwiches in Fancy Shapes

Keep them simple. Young girls usually are not adventurous eaters.

plain white bread
slice of bologna
slice of cheese

Layer these. Use butter if desired. Cut into fancy shapes with canape cutters or small cookie cutters. Arrange on serving plate with cut-up fruit and cheese cubes.

Last Minute Family Dinner

Hamburger-Mashed Potato Pie*
Tossed Salad
Heat and Serve Rolls
Milk-Coffee-Tea-Ice Water
Vanilla Ice Cream with Chocolate Sauce

When you feel God nudging you to invite someone over, don't hold back, just because you only have 60 minutes to prepare dinner. Actually, you could order a take-out pizza, fix a tossed salad and be ready to sit down in half that time, so an hour is plenty.

Maybe you just heard that a friend's husband is out of town, and she and the kids are home alone all week. During a phone call, you learned that a friend had had an especially harrowing day at work — for her, not having to fix dinner could be a godsend.

Listen to the Lord, and be open to offering last-minute invitations. In giving of yourself, you will receive great joy. So make a quick trip to the grocery store and start browning the hamburger!

Hamburger-Mashed Potato Pie

Saute in 2 T. fat: 1 medium onion, chopped
2 lb. ground chuck

Drain the browned meat and mix it with:
2 cans cut green beans, drained
2 cans tomato soup, condensed

Pour into greased casserole.

Spread over top an icing layer of mashed potatoes. (Make instant potatoes while the meat is cooking.)

Bake at 350 degrees for 30 minutes.

Things to Remember for Next Time

14

Don't Forget Yourself!

The "Christian work ethic" can be a hard task-master. How can you be a "good Christian," if you don't keep busy all the time doing something worthwhile? We put this pressure on ourselves and on others, and our judgments come back to haunt us: "Why are you lying around, not accomplishing anything?"

I struggle with this every day. I don't want people to know I took a nap on Sunday afternoon, or that I actually sat and watched a television show, without even doing needlework at the same time. Somewhere inside, I feel I have been wrong if I have not been busy.

In the past, I worked hard to feel good about myself and to make sure others respected me. ("I must be doing something right — they seem impressed!") Work was also a handy way to escape thinking about problems — what was making me unhappy or frustrated. I would just go on my "merry" way, accomplishing good things in spite of the mess inside.

But as I indicated at the outset, that sort of attitude can tie you up in knots. And it is so tiring! You are never doing enough. You are never finished. There is always more work. Somehow, the devil has taken the truth of the pleasure from a job well done and twisted it to make something obsessive and ugly.

But if we are working for the Lord, instead of for ourselves, all that comes into balance. The Lord knows exactly how much Rest & Relaxation we need. And we do need some. He desires to give us time to get refreshed, time to pursue hobbies and special interests. The catch is, are we in close enough contact with Him, to hear His guidance?

I know that, in order to be the woman God wants me to be, I need to work when He directs and rest when He tells me to. Will I pay attention to the nudges He gives me, or do I care more about what other people think? Will I ever learn that no matter how hard I work, I cannot please everybody, and that the only one I really need to please is Jesus?

The secret is to pray. I need to remember and practice this each day, and so do you. Some days we will be better at it than others, but it will definitely be worth the effort.

"Lord, what should I do now?" He will show you when to take a break from cleaning and read a magazine. One day you may sense Him telling you to stop in the middle of dinner preparations to read your daughter a story or call a friend. Do it. Unexpectedly you may feel you should leave the dishes and go outside for a game of basketball with your son. Do it. When you're ironing, you may feel a nudge to set it aside for a talk with your husband. Do it. Before digging into your next task, you may get a nudge to go have a short nap. Do it. These are subtle messages Jesus gives you to stop working and care for yourself, or for those around you.

Often it is easier for us to accept, when it means helping someone else. The trick is to listen when the direction is to take care of yourself. Jesus loves you and wants what is best for you. It might be His perfect will to have you drop everything and go out with your husband or roommate for dinner and a movie. The home may be a little out of shape, but tonight you need a break — time to read a good book or just relax and do some knitting. If you pridefully refuse to rest until all the housework is done, you are in trouble. There is always more to do.

Besides being open to changing your plans, you also need to put time for yourself in your schedule. There are certain things necessary for your own well-being, and they don't just happen; you need to plan them. Make sure your weekly calendar includes daily time set aside for:

1. A Regular Quiet Time. God asks you to have a regular time with Him for prayer and for reading the Bible. It does not have to be lengthy, but it does need to be disciplined. Don't do it just when you feel like it. Set a time: just ten minutes in the morning will make a big difference in how you start your day. Even the most unspiritual Christian will feel cleaner and go into the day ready, after a time alone with God.

2. Personal Hygiene. Bathing, brushing and flossing teeth, make-up, and hair. Maybe you are already disciplined in these areas, but from experience, this is where many people scrimp. I always took care of the house and children first and only did myself, in whatever time was left over. You may do this because you are unhappy about your weight or your looks — "It won't matter what I do; I won't look good anyway!" Possibly you have the idea that Christians should not spend time on themselves or their looks. Depression can be another reason a person chooses to skip personal hygiene: "I'm too unhappy to care how I appear to others."

God had an important lesson to teach me in this area. When I first began to see the reality of Jesus in my life, close friends helped me to see that I needed to be grateful for all He had given me. So what if I was not perfect! I needed to take care of myself and do the best I could with what I had. Two disciplines made a real difference in my life: taking a shower every morning and spending ten minutes applying some light make-up. Maybe you have trouble having a quiet time or doing the ironing, but this is where I faced the need to *choose* to be *obedient*. When I felt lousy about myself, it was easy to give up and say, "Who cares?" But the result was feeling even worse — a vicious circle.

Make the choice to care about yourself — to set out into your day comfortable with how you look.

3. Hobbies. God gives each one of us special gifts and talents. But it takes time to develop skills and to be creative. Set time to do this; it won't just happen, unless you plan for it. If you don't know what to do for this type of relaxation, pray. Look for God's direction. The list is endless — handwork of all types, puzzles, carpentry, gardening, reading, writing, collecting . . . .

What do you like to do, or feel called to do?

What would you like to try or to learn about?

4. Exercise. Lately, it seems exercise is all we hear about. The truth is, we all need some for the sake of our health and well-being. And of all the ways we have of dissipating stress, it is the most beneficial. (Not much good can be said for over-eating or over-sleeping, let alone drugs.) Pray about what is the best exercise for you. Plan for it in your schedule, aiming for 3 to 5 times a week. They say that it should be brisk enough to elevate your pulse above 120, for half an hour at a time. I love to walk. For me, I can exercise and pray out loud at the same time. Others prefer jogging, an exercycle, aerobics, an exercise class, swimming, tennis, or team sports. Check with your doctor first, start off slow, and gradually work into it.

Always be open to God's leading!
No matter what is on your schedule, be willing to drop it —
   To help a friend in need,
   To love a hurting child,
   To talk to your husband when he's discouraged.
The schedule is actually God's — not yours.
He made it.
He knows what is on it.
He knows the needs of all those around you.
He knows what needs to be done and what can wait.
He is always trustworthy.
Ask Him.
He will give you the *discipline* that brings *freedom.*
Only He can maintain the delicate balance.

15

Don't Live in Guilt — Plan to Do It!

There is a *key tool* to make this whole system work: your calendar. You have a weekly schedule and have set months for Big Cleaning and wardrobe update. You plan to do some entertaining and pursue some hobbies and special interests. The calendar brings it all together and keeps you organized.

Purchase a yearly calendar book — small enough to fit in your purse, yet large enough to write notations on each day. I prefer the week-at-a-glance type, in which a week is spread over two pages. Always keep it handy. When you make any kind of commitment, write it down. Check the calendar daily to see what you should be doing. In this way, you will become a person that other people know they can depend on. Also, your mind will not be over-crowded with stray facts, working hard among the clutter to keep things straight. You will be more free to concentrate on what you are doing.

1. Near January 1st, prepare your calendar for the year. Try using a bright marker to note birthdays and anniversaries of close friends and relatives. Use the marker at the top of the page to note special projects that will need attention beginning that week. In this space, I list:

- Big cleaning planning (January 2, July 1)
- Window washing — I put it on April 1 and October 1. This keeps it away from the months I do big cleaning and takes into consideration when the seasons change where I live, so I can raise or lower the storm windows at the same time.
- Putting in the Gardens
- Having a family Christmas picture taken — I need the prints ready by December 1st.
- Wardrobe planning and up-date — March and July
- Planning for summer camps and vacation
- Planning for a graduation party
- Set up physicals or other medical appointments
- Make large purchases (a new rug, for example)

2. As the weeks go by, list all appointments, meetings and parties as soon as they are arranged.

3. Write notes on specific days to jog your memory. Maybe you promised to call a teacher on a certain day for a progress report; write it down. When you write your parents, turn a few weeks further on in the calendar and make a note, reminding yourself to write them again. Are you making a huge pot of soup for an event at church? Put down a reminder to pick up a big pan on Sunday. The library books are due on May 5; turn to that day and write "10 books due." It will save money and return trips for the books you forgot.

Here is a sample of a weekly calendar:

Bright Marker

Wardrobe Planning Ocean City this summer?		March 4 thru March 10
Monday, March 4		**Thursday, March 7**
Make business calls for Doris 4:30 Agenda Meeting 6:30 Bell Choir 7:30 Christian Ed Meeting		John McClurg call Joy's teacher for report 1:00 Go to Hospital with Laurie 3:00 Groceries 7:30 Sharing Group
Tuesday, March 5		**Friday, March 8**
EVAN ROTH 6:30-9:30 School Open House		Gerry Tuckman call D. Abbas & give him my decision 7:30-9:30 Surprise Party for Charlie
Wednesday, March 6	**Saturday, March 9**	**Sunday, March 10**
call school for play tickets 6-7:30 Dinner @ Leverings Clean Basement Do menu & Grocery List	DOROTHY 8:30 High School Registration 12:30 Memorial Service	Marge Palmer 9:00 work in nursery 12:00 Meet with Ron & Amanda 7:30 Cantata 8:30 Sharing Group

Bright Marker means Birthday

Bright Marker — all capital letters means a birthday requiring a gift.

The calendar becomes your plan-ahead diary, a full picture of your commitments. Use it when you sit down to plan your shopping list. It will remind you how much time is available for cooking each day and help you plan accordingly. You will see immediately any needs for birthday cards or gifts for the next week.

So what does the calendar have to do with guilt? We feel guilt, when we forget to do something we have said we would do, but we also experience it when we think we are forgetting something — even when we are uncertain what it is. The devil loves to bog us down with endless lists of things to do, running through our minds. Your calendar is a place to write a job down and then forget about it, until you come to the week it is listed. You are
— not forgetting
— not avoiding
— not procrastinating
You are planning to do the job. The reason for the guilt is erased. Should I worry for weeks about when I will wash the windows? No! I wrote it down in January, for April 1st. At that time I will schedule the job for specific days. My son needs to have the moles on his back checked yearly by a dermatologist. Shall I keep it in the back of my mind all the time, hoping I will "be a good mother" and remember it at some point in the year? Of course not! I write it on a certain week each year and when I turn to that page, I call and make the appointment. What about the new edge molding needed in the family room? John and I are too busy to stain and install it right now. I have a choice: I can worry about when we will ever do it and feel guilty because it is not done or I can turn ahead, find a less crowded week and put down a note to work on it then.

God's plan for us is to have lives full of order, discipline and peace — not guilt, worry and confusion.

What are some jobs, errands, and so on, that you will write on your calendar as reminders, besides those listed?
— Big Cleaning
— Wardrobe planning
— Window washing
—
—
—
—
—
—

PRAYER: Lord, there are so many things I need to do, and so many things I want to do. Help me know what to do first. And then help me follow You step by step, throughout the day. At night, let me rest in You, secure in the knowledge that I have been obedient. Thank You for a schedule and a calendar to help me organize my time and my life. I want to use them as tools to free me to be the person that You have called me to be. Thank you, Lord. Amen.

Epilogue

Congratulations! You have read through the book and have at least a glimpse of how a schedule can make your days run more smoothly. Maybe you have even begun to implement some of the suggestions.

It may seem overwhelming at times — and it is. There is really no way you can keep a house in order all the time. Life just isn't like that. Housekeeping is like life — God asks us to lean on Him — to do our best to keep order, to promote peace, to love those around us. And for you and me, the house is one area where we are tested daily.

I pray that you will feel encouraged about the possibility of getting your house in order, of caring for your family as Jesus wants you to.

Let your hope keep you joyful, be patient in your troubles, and pray at all times.
—Romans 12:12 (TEV)

Appendix A
Monthly Calendar

Sunday	Monday	Tuesday	Wednesday	Thursday	Friday	Saturday

Monthly Calendar

Sunday	Monday	Tuesday	Wednesday	Thursday	Friday	Saturday

Monthly Calendar

Sunday	Monday	Tuesday	Wednesday	Thursday	Friday	Saturday

Monthly Calendar

Sunday	Monday	Tuesday	Wednesday	Thursday	Friday	Saturday

Monthly Calendar

Sunday	Monday	Tuesday	Wednesday	Thursday	Friday	Saturday

Monthly Calendar

Sunday	Monday	Tuesday	Wednesday	Thursday	Friday	Saturday

Monthly Calendar

Sunday	Monday	Tuesday	Wednesday	Thursday	Friday	Saturday

Monthly Calendar

Sunday	Monday	Tuesday	Wednesday	Thursday	Friday	Saturday

Monthly Calendar

Sunday	Monday	Tuesday	Wednesday	Thursday	Friday	Saturday

Monthly Calendar

Sunday	Monday	Tuesday	Wednesday	Thursday	Friday	Saturday

Monthly Calendar

Sunday	Monday	Tuesday	Wednesday	Thursday	Friday	Saturday

Monthly Calendar

Sunday	Monday	Tuesday	Wednesday	Thursday	Friday	Saturday

Appendix B
Weekly Schedule

See pages 46-48.

After setting times and days for your responsibilities on page 48, you will be ready to make out a schedule.

1. First, use light shading to block out the hours you work at a job or have regular commitments outside the home.

2. Next, fill in the regular daily jobs. If you have breakfeast at the same time each day, use a long arrow across the schedule. Do this for all daily jobs. (See page 48.)

3. Then fill in weekly jobs that take blocks of time on specific days (i.e. grocery shopping, laundry, cleaning). Write the item on the correct day along with an approximate time period (1-3, grocery shopping). (See page 48.)

4. Take a look at what time is left. Schedule one or two blocks of time each week for big jobs and special projects. This will be utilized for seasonal jobs, shopping other than groceries, sewing, etc. (See page 48.)

5. Finally, set aside time for yourself — for relaxation, entertainment, and hobbies. (See page 48.)

My Weekly Schedule

Sunday	Monday	Tuesday	Wednesday	Thursday	Friday	Saturday